EMPIRE STATE OF MIND

EMPIRE STATE
OF MIND

HOW JAY-Z WENT FROM
STREET CORNER TO CORNER OFFICE

ZACK O'MALLEY GREENBURG

Portfolio / Penguin

PORTFOLIO / PENGUIN
Published by the Penguin Group
Penguin Group (USA) Inc., 375 Hudson Street, New York, New York 10014, U.S.A. • Penguin Group (Canada), 90 Eglinton Avenue East, Suite 700, Toronto, Ontario, Canada M4P 2Y3(a division of Pearson Penguin Canada Inc.) • Penguin Books Ltd, 80 Strand, London WC2R 0RL, England • Penguin Ireland, 25 St. Stephen's Green, Dublin 2, Ireland (a division of Penguin Books Ltd) • Penguin Books Australia Ltd, 250 Camberwell Road, Camberwell, Victoria 3124, Australia (a division of Pearson Australia Group Pty Ltd) • Penguin Books India Pvt Ltd, 11 Community Centre, Panchsheel Park, New Delhi – 110 017, India • Penguin Group (NZ), 67 Apollo Drive, Rosedale, North Shore 0632, New Zealand (a division of Pearson New Zealand Ltd) • Penguin Books (South Africa) (Pty) Ltd, 24 Sturdee Avenue, Rosebank, Johannesburg 2196, South Africa

Penguin Books Ltd, Registered Offices:
80 Strand, London WC2R 0RL, England

First published in 2011 by Portfolio / Penguin,
a member of Penguin Group (USA) Inc.

10 9 8 7 6 5 4 3 2 1

LIBRARY OF CONGRESS CATALOGING IN PUBLICATION DATA
Greenburg, Zack O'Malley.
   Empire state of mind : how Jay-Z went from street corner to corner office / Zack O'Malley Greenburg.
       p. cm.
   Includes bibliographical references and index.
   ISBN 978-1-59184-381-8
   1. Jay-Z, 1969–   2. Rap musicians—United States—Biography.   I. Title.
   ML420.J29.G74 2011
   782.421649092—dc22
   [B]   2010035334

Printed in the United States of America
Designed by Pauline Neuwirth

For my parents—all three of them—and for Danielle

CONTENTS

EMPIRE STATE OF MIND

Introduction

At 12:10 a.m. on October 4, 1969, Brooklyn's last Myrtle Avenue elevated train rumbled off into the night.[1] Two months later Shawn Corey Carter—better known as Jay-Z—entered the world, making his first home in the nearby Marcy housing projects. The sprawling complex of drab six-story brick buildings today sits five blocks from the Myrtle Avenue line's ghostly remains, a block-long hollow structure that nobody ever bothered to knock down. During Jay-Z's formative years, the rest of Bedford-Stuyvesant was similarly neglected by the authorities; as the drug trade flourished in the 1980s, lessons of supply and demand were never farther than the nearest street corner. Even now, hallmarks of Marcy's past remain: the padlocked metal gates guarding each parking space, the apartment numbers stenciled in white paint beneath street-facing windows to help police catch escaping perpetrators, and, of course, the rusted railway skeleton over Myrtle Avenue, just steps from the platform where the J and Z subways now roll into a modern train station.

The following pages will explain just how Jay-Z propelled himself from the bleak streets of Brooklyn to the heights of the business world. In making that journey, he's gone from peddling cocaine to running multimillion-dollar companies, with worldwide stops at sold-out concerts along the way. Once Jay-Z got going, it took him less than ten years to complete that voyage, thanks to innate talents honed through hustling. His story is the American dream in its purest form, a model for any entrepreneur looking to build a commercial empire.

Jay-Z wouldn't be where he is today were it not for his remarkable abilities as a rhymester and wordsmith. Most hip-hop buffs place him in rap's pantheon, alongside the likes of Rakim, KRS-One, Tupac Shakur, and the Notorious B.I.G. Jay-Z's first album, *Reasonable Doubt*, packs a life's worth of lyrics into a single disc, backed by beats thick with soul and jazz. Though his first album is still considered one of hip-hop's greatest, he garnered criticism for heading in a pop-oriented direction in subsequent efforts. Jay-Z readily admits this was all part of his plan to sell more records. "I dumbed down for my audience, doubled my dollars," he says in one song. "They criticize me for it, yet they all yell, 'Holla.'"[2]

While some of Jay-Z's catchier choruses have drawn the scorn of purists, radio hits like "Hard Knock Life (Ghetto Anthem)" were instrumental in broadening hip-hop's appeal. Jay-Z has helped a cultural movement born amid the ashes of the South Bronx flourish in the fertile fields of the American mainstream. With his aid, hip-hop has gone all the way to the White House— Barack Obama referenced Jay-Z's "Dirt Off Your Shoulder" at a press conference in early 2008 and reportedly called Jay-Z early in his first presidential campaign to ask "what's going on in America."[3] Mid-career classics like *The Blueprint* (2001) and *The Black Album* (2003) earned critical acclaim, and both sold more than two million copies. *The Blueprint 3* (2009) was Jay-Z's eleventh number-one album, breaking Elvis Presley's record for a solo act. At the time of this book's publication, Jay-Z had sold over fifty million records worldwide.[4]

This book's focus is not music, but business, a field in which Jay-Z's prowess rivals his considerable musical talents. He pulled in $63 million in 2010, more than twice as much as the next highest paid hip-hop impresario, Sean "Diddy" Combs.[5] Jay-Z is regularly recognized by *Forbes*, *Fortune*, and others as one of the most successful moneymakers in his industry and beyond. In 2010, he earned more than all but seven CEOs in the country; executives who made less than Jay-Z include Howard Schultz, Michael Dell, and Ralph Lauren.[6]

One of the main reasons for this success is Jay-Z's ability to build and leverage his personal brand. As much as Martha Stewart or Oprah, he has turned himself into a lifestyle. You can wake up to the local radio station playing Jay-Z's latest hit, spritz yourself with his 9IX cologne, slip on a pair of his Rocawear jeans, lace up your Reebok S. Carter sneakers, catch a Nets basketball game in the afternoon, and grab dinner at The Spotted Pig (Jay-Z owns a stake in both) before heading to an evening performance of the Jay-Z–backed Broadway musical *Fela!* and a nightcap at his 40/40 Club. But leave the gold jewelry at home, ditch the baggy shorts and athletic jersey, and don't even think about drinking Cristal: pop-culture arbiter Jay-Z has pronounced all of these items verboten. Instead, consider wearing a platinum Audemars Piguet watch along with a crisp pair of jeans and a dress shirt, preferably by Rocawear, while drinking Armand de Brignac "Ace of Spades" champagne. He'll profit at every step. As he says in one of his songs, "I'm not a businessman—I'm a business, man."[7]

Jay-Z has a nose for money. It drew him away from music and toward the drug trade as a teenager, then back to music as a young adult. In the middle of his career, it took him from the studio to the boardroom, then back to the studio. It's led him to a little bit of both in recent years, creating marketing synergies at every turn. He has a unique ability to set trends and profit from them, and he has milked many of his ventures for astronomical profits. Jay-Z pulled in $204 million for selling his Rocawear clothing line in 2007; the following year, he secured a ten-year, $150-million deal with concert promoter Live Nation at the top of the market. By my estimate—informed by three years of evaluating the fortunes of billionaires and writing about the business of hip-hop for *Forbes*—Jay-Z's personal fortune stands at nearly half a billion dollars. With a little luck, he'll make it to ten figures before his social security checks start to arrive.

Despite Jay-Z's success, there are still many Americans whose impressions of him are foggy, outdated, or down-right incorrect. Over the nine months I spent working on this book, I was astonished at the number of people—mostly middle-aged and white—who, with varying degrees of seri-ousness, advised me to watch my back while writing about a rapper. Perhaps these were simply misguided quips, though I fear that more often than not, they were symptoms of the prejudice that still infects our society. This is not a book about race, but in researching *Empire State of Mind*, I was reminded that Jay-Z's rise is all the more remarkable because of the biases he's been able to overcome.

I've encountered a few people for whom Jay-Z's name doesn't ring a bell, especially in France and Germany, where parts of this book were reported. Every one of them, how-ever, remembered who he was when I identified him as the husband of pop superstar Beyoncé Knowles, the subject of Chapter 8. For the most part, I've been amazed at the number of people with an encyclopedic knowledge of all things Jay-Z. When he declared himself the new Frank Sinatra in his 2009 hit "Empire State of Mind," everybody wanted to weigh in on his bold thesis, from deli proprietors to music industry leaders. "Jay-Z did what most would consider improbable—create an anthem as important to New York as Frank Sina-tra's 'New York, New York,'" Craig Kallman, chief executive of Atlantic Records, told me. "His version is exhilaratingly original and fresh, and captures the essence of today's Big Apple."[8]

In November of 2009, *Newsweek* declared Jay-Z the fourth most important newly minted tycoon of the decade, between hedge fund king John Paulson and Facebook founder Mark Zuckerberg. The honor highlighted his prowess in business and music as well as his cultural impact. "Jay-Z helped change the face of America and its racial politics," declared Russell Simmons, founder of Def Jam Records. "Kids in Beverly Hills now understand the plight of kids in Brooklyn housing projects. Without hip-hop there is no Barack Obama, and without Jay-Z, hip-hop wouldn't be where it is today."[9]

Simmons is a good friend of Jay-Z, and one of many with a great deal of respect for him. I spoke with scores of people who've spent time with Jay-Z, and they all praise his natural brainpower, manifested as much in the shrewdness of his business dealings as in the intricacy of his rhymes. They point out his ability to size people up and rapidly gather information on any situation as it unfolds, both talents honed by years of peddling drugs while skirting rivals and authorities alike. Perhaps most of all, observers note his expansive intellectual curiosity in both music and business.

Though Jay-Z is better known for making and spending money than for giving it away, he has some experience with the latter. He established the Shawn Carter Scholarship Foundation to help underprivileged kids attend college in 2002,[10] donated $1 million to Hurricane Katrina relief in 2005,[11] and joined forces with the United Nations and MTV in 2006 to launch a documentary series called *The Diary of Jay-Z: Water for Life*, which chronicled his journey to Africa to raise awareness about the world water crisis.[12] He also teamed with a slew of celebrities to raise $57 million for Haiti earthquake aid in 2010.[13]

When it comes to his own business dealings, Jay-Z isn't quite so munificent. He has a habit of casting aside his teachers once he's mastered their lessons; to his credit, he isn't on the long list of entertainers who've been taken advantage of by opportunistic friends and family members. On the other hand, this trend has earned him the scorn of a few influential figures in his life, including Marcy mentor Jonathan "Jaz-O" Burks, childhood chum DeHaven Irby, and Roc-A-Fella Records cofounder Damon Dash. Jaz-O, who has known Jay-Z since the mid-1980s, says simply, "His loyalty is to his money."[14]

Jay-Z doesn't like to share the proceeds of projects he feels he can execute on his own, which seems to be one of the reasons he ditched Dash around 2004. I believe it's also the main reason he did not consent to be interviewed for this book. It's an attitude well known by members of his inner sanctum, particularly his shrewd right-hand man John Meneilly, the former accountant who was promoted when Jay-Z and Dash parted ways. (Though Meneilly is essentially a manager, Jay-Z refers to him as a *consigliere*[15]—nobody manages Jay-Z.)

I arranged an appointment with Meneilly to discuss my book in October of 2009, naively assuming he and Jay-Z

would be on board. Upon arriving at Rocawear's headquarters, I was ushered into a high-floor conference room.
In front of a window that revealed a cloudy sunset over lower
Manhattan stood Meneilly, on the phone with somebody
responsible for the logistics of an upcoming concert. What
was so difficult, he asked, about setting up a giant video
screen above the stage to display a ten-minute countdown
sequence right before the start of Jay-Z's show? Eventually the person on the other end relented, and I introduced
myself. As soon as the pleasantries were completed, Meneilly
got right to his main point: "What's in it for us?" That question basically set the tone for the rest of the meeting. If Jay-Z
wasn't going to benefit financially, he wasn't interested in
having a business book written about him by anybody—even
somebody whose *Forbes* articles he'd referenced in at least
three different songs (including the 2007 track entitled "I
Get Money: The Forbes 1-2-3 Remix," featuring 50 Cent and
Diddy).

After spending the better part of a year researching Jay-Z
and familiarizing myself with his tendencies, I can't say I'm
surprised he decided not to cooperate. It's all part of the same
attitude that helped him build his business empire. I'm sure
he figured it wasn't worth granting numerous interviews
when he could instead spend time on a book that he'd profit
from directly. Sure enough, after my meeting with Meneilly,
Jay-Z repurposed the memoir he'd scuttled in 2003[16] and
released his book, *Decoded*, before this one went to press.

In the absence of one-on-one time with Jay-Z, I've stacked

this book with quotes and anecdotes gleaned from my interviews with more than seventy-five people—some on the record, some on background—who've either done business with Jay-Z or are intimately familiar with his life. I've included Jay-Z's own words in the form of published quotes, song lyrics, and stories I gathered from his associates. Some of the people I've interviewed asked me not to include their names in print. Others asked me to remove their contributions from the book altogether after it became clear that Jay-Z wasn't on board with the project. I obliged, even in the case of one particularly well-known producer who received an e-mail from Jay-Z on his BlackBerry in the midst of our interview and showed it to me (the sender was listed in his virtual address book as "Hova").

The coming pages include insights from artists, executives, and acquaintances including the aforementioned DeHaven Irby, Damon Dash, and Jaz-O, and others who've spent considerable time with Jay-Z: DJ Clark Kent, the man who convinced him to stop selling crack and start selling records; Craig Kallman, the CEO of Atlantic Records, which distributed *The Blueprint 3*; Jamal Crawford, the NBA star who played on Jay-Z's first basketball team; Questlove, drummer of the Roots; and Fred "Fab 5 Freddy" Brathwaite, one of hip-hop's most celebrated trailblazers.

Aided by original testimony of these sources and others, along with support from hundreds of television clips and news articles, this book aims to answer a simple question: how did Jay-Z rise from Brooklyn's impoverished housing projects to a position as one of America's most successful business-men? The answer should be of interest to anybody interested in music, sports, or business—and to any entrepreneur in search of a blueprint for building something spectacular from the humblest of beginnings. For that sort of journey, there's no better attitude than Jay-Z's empire state of mind.

1

A Hard Knock Life

It's half past noon, and I'm stuck in a stalled subway just shy of the Flatbush Avenue terminus in Brooklyn, already late to see the man who discovered Jay-Z. I've never met Rodolfo Franklin, better known as DJ Clark Kent; the pictures I've seen of him are from the mid-1990s. What if I don't recognize him? What if he waited for fifteen minutes and left?

When the train finally groans up to the platform, I race out the door, up the stairs, and across the street to Applebee's. A burly man in a black sweat suit is thumbing his BlackBerry on a bench. I glance from his red-and-black Nikes to his matching baseball cap, brim slung low to the left. It's Clark Kent.

"Clark," I begin. "I'm so sorry I'm late. I was . . . the train was—"

"Don't sweat it," he says.

"It just stopped and—"

"Hey, relax." He smiles. The waiter seats us at a table by the window and asks if we'd like to order drinks. Clark Kent orders the Red Apple margarita. "I'm going to need this," he mutters.

I order a plain margarita.

"Strawberry, mango, raspberry, kiwi, or original flavor?"

"Original flavor." The waiter disappears.

"So when did you first meet Jay-Z?" I begin. "Do you remember the first interaction?"

Kent purses his lips and exhales.

"This was when he was about fifteen," he says. "In the Marcy projects. I heard him rap that day, and it was incredible."

"When did you realize that this guy was the next big thing?"

"I realized it back then," he says. "Whenever he rapped with anybody, he outclassed them so bad that I knew it was only a matter of time. I'm no genius for thinking he was incredible, you know what I'm saying? I just saw it early. And I just wanted to do what I could to make it right." The waiter brings out our margaritas, and Kent pauses to take a sip.

"When you grow up in the hood, fast money is all you can think of because of the pressure," he says. "You're in a building with five hundred people when you could be in a house with four. You want to get out. You do whatever you can to get out."

Born on December 4, 1969, Shawn Corey Carter eased his way out of the womb only to start his life in one of Brooklyn's roughest sections. "He was the last of my four children, the only one who didn't give me any pain when I gave birth to him," says his mother, Gloria Carter, in a spoken-word interlude on Jay-Z's *Black Album*. "And that's how I knew that he was a special child."

Within a few years, neighbors in the perilous Marcy Houses were beginning to share that view. At age four, an impatient Jay-Z taught himself how to ride a two-wheel bicycle. He caused a stir when he rode it down the street unaided. "I rode this ten-speed, it was really high," he said in a 2005 interview. "But I put my foot through the top bar, so I'm ridin' the bike sideways and the whole block is like, 'Oh God!' They couldn't believe this little boy ridin' that bike like that. That was my first feeling of being famous right there. And I liked it. Felt good."[1]

Jay-Z's earliest taste of music came around the same time. "My first musical memory had to be, my mom and pop had like a huge record collection," Jay-Z explained at the beginning of the mini-documentary *NY-Z*. "They used to have these parties and [my siblings and I] couldn't come in the front room, so we had to stay in the back. I remember always sneaking out in my pajamas and watching everybody dancing. I mean, we had every record that was out. My mom and pop had great musical taste . . . Michael Jackson, early Jackson Five, Prince early albums, Commodores, Johnson Brothers [*sic*], Marvin Gaye . . . that's soul music."[2]

Had his family maintained this idyllic milieu, Jay-Z might have been on his way to a stellar academic career. "I knew I was witty around the sixth grade," he explained. "I just had that feeling of being smart. We did some tests in the sixth grade, and I was on a twelfth-grade level. I was crazy happy about that. When the test scores came back, that was the first moment I realized I was smart."[3]

But in 1980, Jay-Z's father, Adnis Reeves, abandoned his wife and children. Reeves first left with the goal of tracking down the man who fatally stabbed his brother,[4] but became so consumed with the notion of revenge—and later, by addiction to alcohol and drugs, most notably heroin[5]—that his departure became permanent, leaving Gloria and the children to fend for themselves. For the young Jay-Z, the effects were instantaneous. He was, in his own words, "a kid torn apart once his pop disappeared." His grades declined, and not even his mother could get through to him.[6]

"His pops left when he was like ten," says Clark Kent, whose own father departed when he was a youngster. "That's when you're already believing your father's a superhero, or your father's the best guy in the whole world. And then he leaves, and all of those things become things that hurt you, and make you want to become more into yourself or become more reclusive. And, you know, those things weigh on you."[7]

Jay-Z turned to other male role models like Jonathan "Jaz-O" Burks, an up-and-coming Marcy-based rapper four years his senior. The two first met in 1984 when mutual friends tried to arrange a rap battle between Jaz-O and the young Jay-Z, who was just starting to gain a reputation as a talented lyricist himself. When Jay-Z arrived, the older rapper suggested something a bit less confrontational. "I was like, 'Look, let him rhyme, it doesn't have to be a battle,'" recalls Jaz-O over a telephone interview. "I saw he was a young kid . . . but when he rhymed, I heard something I'd never heard before . . . The cadence, the things that people may have as far as raw talent, but never really pay attention to, he had it."[8]

Almost immediately, the two became good friends. Some observers speculate that Jay-Z's stage name is partly an homage to his mentor and partly a nod to the J and Z subway lines that stop near the Marcy housing projects (Jay-Z insists that his rap name is simply a shortening of his childhood nickname Jazzy, a notion confirmed by DJ Clark Kent). Regardless, Jaz-O's influence was undeniable. Under the elder rapper's tutelage, Jay-Z's lyrics became wittier, his delivery faster, and his syncopation sharper.

"I taught him basic poetic license, metaphor, simile, onomatopoeia—things that most rap artists would say to you, 'What is that?'" remembers Jaz-O. "I taught him that in order to be the best, you don't have to outwardly hone your craft. But in privacy, hone your craft. People don't have to know how hard you work to get something." Aside from musical guidance, Jaz-O and other friends helped provide Jay-Z with basic necessities when his single mother of four couldn't. "I think quite honestly, his situation was a bit dire," says Jaz-O. "He used to go to [his friend] Chase's house often, just so he could eat. My house as well."

≡

Even with Jaz-O's companionship and guidance, Jay-Z remained stung by his father's departure. In a rare moment of vulnerability, he told *Rolling Stone* that his father's exit scarred him so badly that he started to distance himself emotionally from potentially hurtful situations. "I changed a lot. I became more guarded. I never wanted to be attached to something and get that taken away again," he said. "I never wanted to feel that feeling again."[9]

In the ensuing years, the young Jay-Z indeed became troublingly detached. The worst manifestation of this occurred at age seventeen, when Jay-Z shot his drugged-out older brother in the shoulder for stealing a ring.[10] He describes the incident on his second album: "Saw the devil in your eyes, high off more than weed / Confused, I just closed my young eyes and squeezed."[11]

Moments after he fired the shot, Jay-Z raced over to Jaz-O's Marcy apartment and breathlessly explained what had happened. "He was like, 'I shot my brother,'" recalls Jaz-O. "I was like, 'What the fuck did you shoot him for?' He's like, 'I told him to stop taking my stuff.' He said it was kind of an accident . . . he was trying to scare [his brother], but the situation got kind of crazy, and he just happened to hit him in his arm." Though Jay-Z's brother was taken to a nearby hospital for treatment, he never incriminated his younger sibling for the injury. In fact, the pair quickly reconciled, as Jay-Z explains in verse: "Still, you asked to see me in the hospital the next day / You must love me."[12]

Surprisingly, the young rapper's actions didn't result in any serious legal consequences. That may seem unusual, but in the early 1980s, Bedford-Stuyvesant was one of the many poor enclaves in New York that were largely neglected by the authorities. Hospitals were accustomed to admitting victims of stray shots, and Jay-Z's brother didn't want to incriminate a family member. "His brother didn't press charges partly because his brother knew he was wrong," says Jaz-O. "And, you know, they're still brothers. For the most part, he felt to an extent that it was an accident. He understood that it was his little brother who couldn't beat his big brother and was just trying to intimidate him."

The incident revealed a striking similarity between the adolescent Jay-Z and his absent father: an inability to control vengeful impulses. Adnis Reeves's desire to track down his brother's killer led him to abandon his family; Jay-Z's need for retribution was so powerful that he shot his own brother. Perhaps the most compelling part of Jay-Z's lyrical confession is his admission that, all along, he was hoping his brother would try to talk him down ("Gun in my hand, told you step outside / Hoping you said no, but you hurt my pride"[13]). It shows a desire for the sort of discipline that he would eventually learn to impose on himself.

Not surprisingly, unloading a bullet into his brother's shoulder is a moment that Jay-Z would rather forget. In the rare cases when an interviewer brings it up, the rapper maneuvers away from the subject. "I wouldn't feel comfortable talking about that on TV, it's not cool," Jay-Z said in 2002. "That's a bit over the line."[14] Indeed, firing that gun wouldn't be the last time he allowed his desire for revenge to cloud his judgment. As Jay-Z admits in one of his songs, he "had demons deep inside that would raise when confronted."[15]

Despite the magnitude of Jay-Z's struggles at home, few of his peers at Brooklyn's George Westinghouse High School knew the extent of his struggles. "He was very quiet and dressed nice from what I remember," recalls Carlos R. Martinez, who overlapped with Jay-Z at Westinghouse and currently works as a corrections officer in Brooklyn. "That's about it."[16] The mogul-to-be was soft-spoken, except when he was rapping. "He was a clever rapper but not very into talking about it," remembers Billy Valdez, a classmate who's now a music producer in New Jersey. "He did his thing on the low, very humble."[17]

Jay-Z's classmates were too busy dealing with their own problems to speculate on the home life of the quiet kid with a gift for rhyme. In those days, Westinghouse was among the most dangerous schools in New York. Salvador Contes attended Westinghouse at the same time as Jay-Z and went on to teach for thirteen years at the school. He remembers broken windows, smoky stairwells, and a general fear for one's personal safety. "When you went into the boys' bathroom, there were no lights. You'd walk in there, pitch-dark, and you knew things were going on in the bathroom, but you couldn't see," he says. "You didn't want to take a chance. You could have gotten mugged in the bathroom, and you wouldn't have known who did it . . . So you did your best to hold it."[18]

Jay-Z dodged danger by spending most of his time loitering in the school's brightly lit cafeteria. There, he practiced his rap skills by freestyling to beats pounded out on the table. His classmates began to take notice. "You'd always see him in the same spot when you walked into the cafeteria, if you walked in on the left side," Contes remembers. "Literally all the time." There, he'd partake in verbal jousting matches with other aspiring rappers—Westinghouse alums include the Notorious B.I.G. and Busta Rhymes—while his classmates looked on. "It was always a battle on who was better," says Contes. "It was almost disappointing when they didn't do it."

Jay-Z never graduated from high school, thanks in part to the influence of childhood friend DeHaven Irby, who lived across the hall from him in the Marcy projects. The two boys walked to school together every day. They also frequented Brooklyn's asphalt basketball courts. "He wasn't aggressive," recalls DeHaven, now a thickset ex-con, over milk shakes at Dallas BBQ in downtown Brooklyn. "He had a shot, but he wasn't, like, a ballplayer. Seemed like he'd do a lot of studying before he'd make a move. I guess that works for him now."[19]

In 1988, DeHaven relocated to Trenton, New Jersey, to live with his aunt. His basketball coach at Westinghouse suggested he make the move so that he could play at the local high school in Trenton, which had a better program than Westinghouse. But DeHaven dropped out as soon as he saw the lucrative opportunities offered by drug dealing. With a business partnership in mind, he reached out to his old friend Jay-Z.

"I was like, 'Yo, I need you here with me, there's money here, we can get this money,'" says DeHaven. "I had everything already laid out for him before he even came. I already had told everybody in Trenton about him. I used to tell them he was my [biological] brother." [20]

So the eighteen-year-old Jay-Z started taking the train to Trenton on weekends. Eventually, DeHaven's family got used to having him around; before long, he moved in full-time. Jay-Z's mother didn't stop him. "I was already out on my own at fifteen, sixteen years old," says Jay-Z. "My mom didn't put me out, but she did the best thing for me. She allowed me to search. She gave me a long leash." [21]

Jay-Z took that freedom and used it to start picking up what one might call a practical education. DeHaven taught Jay-Z everything he knew about the heady local drug market—as Jay-Z himself said, "DeHaven introduced me to the game" [22]—and soon he was on the streets selling cocaine. He developed a strict profit-making policy, one that the locals quickly noticed. "They knew he was about business," remembers DeHaven. "No shorts, meaning he was getting all his money. All the money. If the product was ten dollars, you couldn't get it for nine dollars . . . a lot of people thought of him as being stingy."

Even as he started getting involved in the drug trade, Jay-Z made time for music. In 1988, Jaz-O became the first rapper to land a deal with British label EMI. When the company flew him to London for two months to record his album, he brought along Jay-Z and a young producer named Irv "Gotti" Lorenzo, who'd go on to found Murder Inc., a record label that gained success and notoriety in the late 1990s. "I treated him and Irv as equals, but [Jay-Z] was basically my sidekick," recalls Jaz-O. "It was his first exposure to traveling and doing things in the music industry." Shortly after his nineteenth birthday, Jay-Z got his first real taste of luxury when he cruised to the London release party for Jaz-O's album on New Year's Eve in a Cadillac limousine.

Upon returning to the United States, Jay-Z talked his way onto the tour bus of Big Daddy Kane, a successful rapper from hip-hop's golden age in the late 1980s and early 1990s. A host of hip-hop luminaries joined Kane on tour, including Queen Latifah, MC Serch, Shock G, and a young Tupac Shakur. As a member of Kane's posse, Jay-Z would sometimes go onstage during intermissions to entertain crowds with his spitfire freestyle delivery. Though Jay-Z today grosses over $1 million per show, he spent four months in 1989 working the hip-hop equivalent of an unpaid internship—rapping for room and board, which consisted of a spot on the tour bus floor and a free pass at the buffet.

MC Serch, whose real name is Michael Berrin, recalls Jay-Z having to ask Kane for money to go to a local burger joint for dinner. His memories of Jay-Z were not that different from those of the young rapper's high school classmates. "I just remember Jay having gold teeth in his mouth, having a big smile, not saying a lot. Jay wasn't a big talker," he says. "Kane rolled with the realest of the real dudes from Brooklyn. And Jay was just one of these young gunners that rolled with him."[23]

After the tour, Jay-Z found himself between worlds. Nearly twenty years old, he'd gotten a taste of the good life with Jaz-O in London, and he'd rubbed elbows with the biggest names in hip-hop on Big Daddy Kane's tour. But he'd dropped out of high school, and his own musical career hadn't gotten to a point where he could make serious money as an artist. So he picked up where he'd left off as a hustler. "I think he realized that in order to really push the music, you needed to be able to finance yourself," says Jaz-O. "He chose to quite simply get money, as most of us did in our circle, we just chose to get money and get out of the hood any way we could."

Specifically, Jay-Z went back into business with DeHaven. From a supply and demand standpoint, the decision made a lot of sense. In the 1980s, New York was the main East Coast entry point for cocaine imports from South America. With ties in New York and Trenton, Jay-Z and DeHaven did what any shrewd businessmen would do with a growing enterprise: they expanded into undeveloped markets in Maryland and Virginia, where the competition was lighter and the clientele less sophisticated. "New York was the capital of drugs," explains DeHaven. "This is where it came in, back then. So the further you were away from here, the higher [the price] goes."

Jay-Z would later use his music to boast that he wasn't just selling $10 crack rocks on the corner. In "Takeover" he says, "I was pushing° weight back in '88,"[24] a slang-driven lyric meant to emphasize the magnitude of his dealings. "There wasn't no nickel and diming around back then," says DeHaven with a chuckle. "There was money in the streets. It wasn't a recession. It was Reaganomics."

Even as Jay-Z's partnership came to be interrupted by DeHaven's intermittent prison stints, he continued moving back and forth between Brooklyn, Trenton, and locations farther south with the help of other associates—and the rise of a new and profitable product: crack cocaine. Dreamed up somewhere in Colombia during the mid-1980s, the process of creating crack could be completed by anyone with a coffeemaker, a hot plate, some cocaine powder, and a few common grocery items. If diluted with another additive like baking soda, a brick of cocaine powder could produce enough $10 crack rocks to quadruple a street dealer's profits.[25]

Though Jay-Z's music admittedly "came second to moving this crack,"[26] his collaborations with Jaz-O continued. In 1990, the pair released a song called "The Originators," following it with a music video in which Jay-Z sports a Waldoesque red-and-white-striped shirt. Neither the blithe ballad nor the campy video delved into the grim urban subject matter that characterized both Jay-Z's life at the time and much of his later work; on the contrary, "The Originators" evoked the playful boasts of early records like Sugarhill Gang's "Rapper's Delight." What set Jay-Z apart as an artist was the sharpness and rapidity with which he delivered his lyrics; that verbal dexterity earned Jay-Z some attention in the underground hip-hop scene. It also served as a moneymaking alibi. With his underground and underworld profiles on the rise, Jay-Z would sometimes help his mother financially—or splurge on extravagances like gold teeth. In the song "December 4th" he says, "I hit my momma with cash from a show that I had, supposedly." In other words, he was using unpaid musical appearances as a front to hide the fact that most of his money came from selling drugs.

"The difference between him and a lot of other people is you really couldn't tell that he was this guy that had a whole bunch of money from being in the streets because he wasn't out there buying Benzes," says Kent. "He was doing little things, like, you know, a little Lexus here, but he was buying a Lexus when all these guys in the street were buying Benzes and BMWs. To be smart enough to play yourself down to just keep the paper means you're doing business properly. And Jay-Z was always about keeping the paper."

These days, some question Jay-Z's drug-dealing résumé and challenge his street cred. DeHaven, who hasn't spoken with Jay-Z since their falling-out in the late 1990s, doesn't deny the rapper's involvement in the drug scene. However, he suggests that many of Jay-Z's lyrical depictions of hustling were really stories borrowed from his own life—and that Jay-Z distanced himself because he didn't want people to know. "I've been around one of the greatest sellers in the world, whether the story was real or not," says DeHaven with a smile that betrays a hint of nostalgia. "An O.G. [original gangster] explained it to me on that level. He said, 'If Jay was ever jealous or he ever wanted to be you, what purpose is there to have you around? 'Cause then people could see who's who.' Like, 'The person you rap about seems to be [DeHaven].'" Still, one person who spent time with both Jay-Z and DeHaven during the early 1990s estimates that Jay-Z was moving a kilogram of cocaine (a $12,000 value[27] before the fourfold street markup) per week. "He was definitely involved in the narcotics game," says the source, who asked to remain anonymous. "There's no denying that."

In 1992, Jay-Z's musical prospects got a boost when Atlantic Records hired Clark Kent. As part of the artists and repertoire (A&R) department, Kent was charged with scouting new talent. His mind immediately flashed back to the youngster he'd met in the Marcy projects years earlier. But now that Jay-Z was a successful drug dealer, he was hard to track down. Kent was eventually able to get Jay-Z's number from a friend. "The conversation was, 'Yo, I'm over here at Atlantic Records, we gotta do this.' He's like, 'Nah, I'm good,'" Kent remembers. "And then daily, for two months or so, I'm like, 'Yo, I'm over at Atlantic Records, we gotta do this.' It was still a lot of, 'Yeah, aight, whatever.'"

Jay-Z remained hesitant to devote time to music that could

be spent making more money hustling. But after continuous prodding, Kent finally convinced him to appear on a remix, then on a song called "Can I Get Open" with a group called Original Flavor in 1993. "I convinced him, unwillingly," says Kent. "He was like, 'I'm not spending money to do this. If it happens, it happens, but I'm going to be doing what I gotta do, so it's only going to happen when I come up from down south.'"

Jay-Z's reluctance to splurge on music was understandable, as there are a lot of people to pay when recording a hip-hop song. There's the producer, who uses an array of gizmos including drum machines, synthesizers, and a technique called "sampling" to create the basic repeating element, or "hook," of the song. Samples are elements of previously recorded songs—perhaps the horns from a soul record or the snare drum from an old jazz standard, or occasionally the entire song minus the original vocals—and are often used to help create a song's musical backbone, known as the "beat" or the "track." In the mid-1990s, a producer might charge $5,000 per song plus a 50 percent share in the rights to the song, which translates to a 3 to 4 percent royalty on a whole album (on top of that, the use of a single sample might cost $5,000 to $15,000, plus an additional royalty cut[28]). The rapper, also known as the MC or emcee, records vocals over the beat. Once the lyrics are added, sound engineers adjust volume levels and add effects to complete the process. Postproduction and promotion add to the tab, as does studio time—as much as $2,500 per hour for a minimum of four hours during the period in which Jay-Z first started recording.[29]

Kent, a veteran producer, hoped that with enough songs under his belt, Jay-Z would be able to impress Atlantic or another label enough to get a record deal to fund future recordings. To that end, he persuaded Jay-Z to record a song with a rapper named Sauce Money. At the time, Kent and Sauce were working with a production company called 3-D Enterprises owned by former NBA star Dennis Scott. Patrick Lawrence, a 3-D employee and producer known professionally as A Kid Called Roots, was in charge of booking studio time for Kent, Sauce, and Jay-Z. Though the song never made it onto anybody's album in the end, Lawrence remembers the impression Jay-Z left on him during the session. "Jay-Z was a street dude who didn't realize how talented he was," recalls Lawrence between bites of garlic naan at a Manhattan eatery. "He thought it was like, 'If it was really that complicated, it wouldn't be that easy for me.' So he didn't take it serious. It was Clark Kent who said, 'You need to go hard with this,' and convinced him to fall back on the street thing and go full steam with the music."

When Jay-Z arrived to record his verse, he hadn't yet heard the beat. Instead of asking to hear it or practicing his verse, he started joking around with Sauce, much to Lawrence's chagrin. Though Lawrence had heard rumors that Jay-Z memorized all his verses in lieu of writing them down, nothing was getting done and he was getting antsy. "I'm thinking to myself, 'This guy hasn't written his song, nobody's heard his verse or anything like that,'" recounts Lawrence. "We've been here for three hours, and they've just been laughing and talking about stuff and haven't been talking about music. So I finally was like, 'Jay, come on, man, you gotta fucking lay your vocals, man. This is on my ass, I'm wasting studio time, I'm almost over budget!' Everybody's like, 'Oh, this guy's getting feisty.' So [Jay says], 'Okay, let me hear the song.'"[30]

Lawrence played the track. Jay-Z began mumbling along to it, then picked up a pen and a notebook and seemed to start scribbling notes. He placed the pad on the sofa and started pacing back and forth, muttering more half-formed words. After five minutes, he glanced once more at the pad and told Lawrence he was ready. While Jay-Z was in the sound booth recording his verse, Lawrence went over to see what he'd written in the notebook, which was still sitting on the couch. "I walk to the pad, and there's fucking nothing on it," Lawrence recalls. "He was doing it as a fucking joke, like just to show people. That was when I was like, 'This guy is the best rapper.'"

Brilliant rapper though he was, Jay-Z continued to hustle. The decision was part of a business philosophy that can be boiled down to a very simple rule: focus on whatever venture offers the most realistic opportunity to make the most money. Early on, that meant selling drugs; Jay-Z saw music as a fun side project, or perhaps a way to diversify his revenue streams. "His first album was supposed to be his only album . . . at least that's what he said," notes Touré, who authored *Rolling*

Stone's 2005 cover story on the rapper. "I think that was real in his mind. He was like, 'This is a pay cut.'"³¹

It would take more than a nudge to make Jay-Z change his attitude. According to DeHaven, that came suddenly and violently sometime in 1994. "He saw death," DeHaven explains. "He saw the bad side of the game. He almost had his life taken. And that's what did it. He messed with the wrong people." Jaz-O recalls the same incident: "When he saw the individual [preparing to shoot], he ran for his life, which he should have. A couple of shots fired, but the gun jammed and that's what saved his life."

Both DeHaven and Jaz-O take credit for the fact that Jay-Z's assailant never came after their friend again. Jaz-O claims he used street diplomacy to snuff out the dispute, which he says was sparked by "dirty dealings" (he wouldn't elaborate). DeHaven implies something a bit more direct. "How did he ever think them people stopped looking for him?" he says, grinning ominously. "That was me all along." Though Jay-Z himself has never confirmed or denied that either Jaz-O or DeHaven served as a guardian angel, he has said that he stopped dealing in the mid-1990s after being ambushed by rival drug dealers: "I had near brushes, not to mention three shots, close range, never touched me, divine intervention."³²

Clark Kent doesn't believe those experiences were what caused Jay-Z to stop hustling. "That shit don't mean nothing," he says. "Getting shot at is something that you expect when you're in the street hustling . . . Shit, I got shot at, you know what I'm saying? You're going to get shot. You're going to get shot at. And if you live, it's all good. That just meant he lived to hustle another day. It wasn't that. What I think changed him and made him say he was going to commit [to music] was the success of that first record."

Jay-Z has admitted that a number of factors led to his decision to stop hustling. "It wasn't specifically one thing," he told the *Washington Post* in 2000. "It was more so out of fear. You can't run the streets forever. What are you going to be doing when you're thirty years old, or thirty-five or forty? I had a fear of being nothing—that pretty much drove me."[33] For the burgeoning businessman, the decision to stop dealing sometime around 1995 could also be explained as a simple recalibration of risks and benefits. "When he saw the money that he could make in the music business," Touré muses, "and be legal with it, and not have to worry about the police, and getting shot by other drug dealers, and all the other predators who'd been coming at him, it made a lot of sense."[34]

Jay-Z explains his thought process in verse: "I sold kilos of coke, I'm guessing I could sell CDs."[35] As usual, he proved to be a quick study. He would find his primary instructor in that field when Kent introduced him to a young Harlem entrepreneur named Damon Dash.

"If they were still together," says Kent, "they'd be billion-aires."

2

The Roc-A-Fella Dynasty

ust as Bill Gates dropped out of Harvard to start Microsoft, one could say that Jay-Z left the Damon Dash
school of business to start his own ventures—but not
before building an unparalleled commercial hip-hop empire
encompassing music, film, liquor, and a clothing company
that grew from a few sewing machines into a giant that produced $700 million in annual revenues.[1]

During that time, Jay-Z's erstwhile business partner lived
like a modern Louis XIV and sported an attitude to match.
"I am trying to take over the whole world," Dash declared in
2003. "I want a billion dollars after tax."[2] The stocky, bald-
headed dynamo once boasted a butler, a personal chef, and a
glass-roofed limo. He purchased pricey dwellings around the
world and stocked them with hundreds of pairs of shoes he'd

never wear. Shortly after he and Jay-Z parted ways in 2004, the cash evaporated, and so did the lifestyle.

These days, you usually don't find Damon Dash unless he wants you to. So when, after trying no fewer than ten different numbers for him, I heard his voice on the other end of the line, he seemed just as startled as I was.

"How did you get this number?"

"Spent two months asking everybody I know."

"I must be getting sloppy."

Perhaps because he was impressed, perhaps because he was startled, perhaps because he had an ax to grind, he started telling me the tale of how it all began.

"Me, Jay . . . we all did illegal things," he began. "And we found a way to make it in the industry."[3]

In 1994, Dash was managing a group called Future Sound and making money as a party promoter. He generated hype for his events by handing out free bottles of champagne to the first one hundred women to enter; everyone else had to pay a cover charge. Clark Kent noticed that flair for marketing and decided that all Dash needed was a top-line talent to promote. He suggested a meeting with Jay-Z, but the Harlem-based Dash was skeptical at first.

"He couldn't believe there was this Brooklyn guy who was this good," recalls Kent. "He was, like, scared to go to Brooklyn, 'cause all he thinks is stickup artists and killing. And when I introduced him [to Jay], the first thing he did was see he was wearing [Nike] Air Force 1s and was like, 'Hold up, this guy is cool.' So he got it immediately, and they were cool, and then he heard Jay rhyming."

Just as Jaz-O and Clark Kent had been wowed by Jay-Z's lyrical prowess, so, too, was Damon Dash. With Dash on board as Jay-Z's business partner, the rapper released the single "I Can't Get with That" in 1994, complete with shout-outs to Dash and Kent. By the end of 1995, Jay-Z had recorded the bulk of what would eventually become his first album, *Reasonable Doubt.* Thanks to his well-connected friends, Jay-Z was able to land tracks from some of the most highly esteemed producers in hip-hop: Clark Kent, DJ Ski, and—perhaps most impressive of all—DJ Premier, also known as Primo.

"Getting on a Primo beat at the time Jay-Z got on a Primo beat for the first time was the equivalent of driving a Ferrari or something like that," says Elizabeth Mendez Berry, who has interviewed Jay-Z extensively and is now an adjunct professor at New York University's Clive Davis Department of Recorded Music. "It was a moment of arriving."[4]

With Jay-Z's debut album nearly complete, he and Dash shopped it to all the major record labels, but there were no takers. They couldn't even get a deal at Atlantic Records, where Clark Kent had the ear of key decision makers. "They just didn't get it," says Kent. "The reality of what he was talking about was a little too much for the people in the company. There were people who were doing reality rap, but they weren't doing *his* reality rap. A lot of what [Jay] said went over a lot of people's heads. When you hear NWA, you hear gun killin', drug sellin', but you hear it in such a very plain English that when you get this guy who's extremely crafty with words, he's probably going all the way over your head. And he's saying it in a way that you have to practically be a drug dealer to understand it." Entertainment lawyer Donald David believes the major labels turned Jay-Z down for a different reason. "They were scared of the violence," he says. "There was still the East-West rivalry concept, and people were a little bit concerned about the content and lyrics of his music. The stuff was pretty rough stuff."[5]

So Jay-Z and Dash pooled their resources with a silent partner, Kareem "Biggs" Burke, to start their own record label, Roc-A-Fella Records. They picked the name to signify wealth on the level of John D. Rockefeller, the world's first billionaire, and to evoke images of the Rockefeller family's enduring dynasty. In typically ironic fashion ("Jay-Z is the king of the double entendre," says Kent), the name of the record label founded in part with Jay-Z's cocaine-dealing profits was also a clever jab at New York's draconian Rockefeller drug laws.

"These guys started up the pressing of their own records, their CDs, their T-shirts, their stickers, their flyers, with their own money," recalls producer Patrick "A Kid Called Roots" Lawrence. "Where that money came from? I knew it didn't come from a label. It came out of their own pockets. And we know that they didn't work at Target."[6]

They began peddling music from the backs of their cars,

Jay-Z from his trademark white Lexus, Dash from his Nissan Pathfinder. They traversed the five boroughs of New York, distributing Jay-Z's tracks in clubs and on street corners, using the same hustling skills Jay-Z learned as a drug dealer. To say they sold music in a few unorthodox locations is an understatement.

"We were going to barbershops! You name it, we was there," recalls Dash. "The energy was definitely there, you know? Like I said, I could see myself working with him in the future. We made a pact to do what we had to do." To that end, Jay-Z kept releasing more singles in an effort to build on his burgeoning popularity. In early 1996, he put out a song called "Ain't No Nigga"; a seventeen-year-old Foxy Brown sang the catchy hook. "Within three months," recalls rapper-turned-businessman Michael "Serch" Berrin, "that record was the hottest record in New York."[7]

Jay-Z helped fuel his growing legend—that of the slick kingpin-turned-rapper—at open microphone nights such as Mad Wednesdays, a weekly unsigned artist showcase in Manhattan. He wowed crowds by deftly delivering lyrics like "I got extensive hoes with expensive clothes / And I sip fine wines and spit vintage flows"[8] and by crafting clever songs like "Twenty-Two Twos," in which he repeats the words *two*, *to*, and *too* a total of twenty-two times in the first verse. "Jay before he got [big] was a totally different person than he is now. He was hungry," Dash remembers. "He was willing to quit hustling, he was willing to do whatever it took."

At the time, Jay-Z claimed he was only in for one album,

and that he would go back to the more lucrative occupation of hustler after he finished. Those who spent time with him in the mid-1990s say it was all part of his marketing plan. With the hype growing around Jay-Z and Roc-A-Fella Records, Jay-Z was able to land a distribution deal with Will Soco-lov's Freeze Records in partnership with California-based Priority Records. Under the terms of the deal, Roc-A-Fella would handle the production and promotion, and Freeze and Priority would handle the manufacturing and sales of the finished product; they also gained control of the mas-ters. Profits would be split down the middle. "Back then, the standard royalty was 20 percent, or two dollars per album," says David. "To have a deal where you're splitting the profits fifty-fifty is far more beneficial for the artist. Jay-Z was very smart to do what he did."

By the time Jay-Z and Dash landed their first deal, they'd built up so much underground buzz about Jay-Z's music that the gritty *Reasonable Doubt* sold 420,000 copies in its first year.[9] Counting copies sold informally on the street, Serch estimates that the real number was closer to 800,000. But when Jay-Z went to collect his paycheck, he got his first taste of corporate bureaucracy.

"Will Socolov gave him the whole corporate label bullshit: 'I don't have the money, you've got to wait,' this and that," Serch recounts. "At that time, now everybody was barking up Jay's door. He's got all these records sold, and he's owed all this money, and he's not getting his money from Freeze. So he says, 'All right, I've got to get off this label.' And negotiated his release, but negotiated it with his masters. So he got to keep his masters, which was unheard of. For an independent artist to leave a label? He always seemed to be unique and special."[10]

Out of desperation to get signed, most artists give away a huge percentage of the rights to their music upon receiving their first record deal. Those who are fortunate enough to hang on to their songs—or buy the catalogs of other musicians—often cash out to make a quick buck later on. Michael Jackson, who shrewdly added a massive chunk of the Beatles' catalog to his own in 1984, was forced to sell a 50 percent stake in the catalog to Sony ten years later for $90 million. The deal, prompted by Jackson's creditors, turned out to be a disaster: at the time of Jackson's death in 2009, the catalog's worth was estimated at $1.5 billion, valuing Jackson's half at $750 million.[11]

Dash advised Jay-Z to try and get back the rights to his music, something few artists figure out until later in their career, if at all. "Own your masters, slaves!" Jay-Z exhorts his fellow musicians in one song.[12] In the case of *Reasonable Doubt*, Jay-Z's recovery of his masters was possible both because his complaint was valid and because he was willing to confront Socolov—something a meeker artist might be scared to do for fear of getting dropped. Kent attributes Jay-Z's boldness to the experience he gained on the street dealing with characters even more ruthless than record label executives.

"If you did it in the streets, and you did your business properly in the streets, and you made good money in the streets, when you walk into a boardroom you look at everybody in the boardroom like they're suckers," Kent explains. "So you know that it's not going to be hard for you to master the boardroom if that's what you want to do. You ran the streets. You mastered guys trying to kill you and guys trying to take over your block."

Even if Jay-Z hadn't been able to get his masters back, his deal was for only one album. He made the arrangement deliberately so that he'd be free to pursue another more lucrative deal if his career took off. "That was the smartest thing he ever did. The label knew he was talented, but they didn't know how talented," says Lawrence. "Everybody does a two-album, three-album, four-album, seven-album deal. Nine times out of ten, the label wants to lock you in for life . . . Having that one-off allowed him to be free." Serch believes Jay-Z also benefited from the help of a strong supporting cast. "He had very arrogant businessmen around him, that were providing him excellent information, helping him make good decisions."

With the masters in their possession, Jay-Z and Dash were able to sell *Reasonable Doubt* for a second run. This time, they had a bidding war on their hands—not just for the rights to publish the second run of *Reasonable Doubt*, but to sign the ascendant rapper for his next album. In 1996, Jay-Z and Dash mulled offers from Sony and a somewhat smaller one from Def Jam Recordings; they eventually chose the latter because of its reputation as the home of hip-hop. The deal called for Def Jam (now part of NBC Universal) to purchase a 33 percent stake (published reports incorrectly pegged it at 50 percent) in Roc-A-Fella Records for $1.5 million; the label also acquired a portion of the rights to Jay-Z's future master recordings. Def Jam would cover all production costs for Jay-Z's albums and videos, and they'd share the profits with Roc-A-Fella. But because Def Jam owned only a third of Roc-A-Fella instead of the usual fifty-fifty split, they also took just a third of the profits. Thanks to stubborn negotiating from Dash, this left the Roc-A-Fella trio with 67 percent of the gains instead of 50 percent, a difference that would add up to millions of dollars once Jay-Z's music really started to sell.[13]

"I think Jay learned a lot from Dame," muses Kent. "If you're down with somebody who's doing smart things, you become smarter instantly, because you watch the smart things. You might figure your own way to do the smart things, but if you see it, you understand it." Russell Simmons, the cofounder of Def Jam, sees Dash's role in Jay-Z's career as even more crucial. "The thing you have to understand about [Dash] is, he thought the whole thing up," Simmons told *New York* magazine in 2006. "Jay-Z just came from Damon's imagination. The man is a visionary."[14]

With the Def Jam–backed Roc-A-Fella label officially established, Jay-Z embarked upon a rigorous recording schedule. Though the edgy *Reasonable Doubt* had proven to be a worthy debut, Jay-Z decided to soften his sound to draw a wider audience. So he turned to Sean "Diddy" Combs to produce his second album, *In My Lifetime, Vol. I*, in 1997. The album was distinctly slicker than Jay-Z's debut, and it earned a lukewarm response from critics who preferred the rapper's Brooklyn grit. *Rolling Stone* called it "a corrective measure in the opposite direction as *Reasonable Doubt*, bearing all the marks of an artist with his eye on a larger pop prize, to the detriment of his art."[15] Still, *In My Lifetime* quickly earned platinum status and more cash for the Roc-A-Fella partners.

It wasn't until Jay-Z's third album, *Vol. 2 . . . Hard Knock Life*, that his career exploded. The title track, an infectious ditty that sampled a song from the Broadway musical *Annie*, burned across the summer's airwaves and was eventually named the eleventh best hip-hop song of all time by VH1.[16] The album sold five million copies in the United States alone,[17] but hip-hop purists lamented that the rapid-fire lyricist had slowed down his rhymes—in terms of both speed and nuance—to appeal to a pop audience. Well aware of the shift, Jay-Z made no apologies: "Truthfully, I wanna rhyme like [rapper] Common Sense, but I did five mil / I ain't been rhyming like Common since."[18]

From a business perspective, moving toward the mainstream was the right decision. The nature of Jay-Z's Roc-A-Fella/Def Jam deal gave him added incentive to make albums with mass appeal. Whereas most artists would only see royalties of about $1 or $2 per copy sold, the joint venture earned Jay-Z closer to $3 or $4 per copy[19]—meaning he made $15 to $20 million on his third album alone. His career as a hustler was over.

Jay-Z's hustler's instinct was a different matter. After the meeting with *Rolling Stone*'s Touré in 1997, Jay-Z offered to drive the writer home to Brooklyn. They walked to Jay-Z's Range Rover; the rapper hopped into the passenger side, his driver slid behind the wheel. When Touré opened the door and sat down in back, Jay-Z twitched and turned back to him. "He said, 'Where I come from, we don't usually let anybody sit behind us,'" Touré recalls. "He knows I'm not going to fucking shoot him. But . . . I think that hustler's instinct is still there within him, and will always be."

That inclination may have been the driving force behind a highly publicized incident in December of 1999. Just weeks before the release of Jay-Z's fourth album, *Vol. 3 . . . The Life and Times of S. Carter*, a brawl broke out in the VIP section of the Kit Kat Club in Manhattan's Times Square. Amid the scuffle, Jay-Z confronted record producer and onetime friend Lance "Un" Rivera, who'd been rumored to be bootlegging copies of *Life and Times* after coproducing the song "Dope Man" on the album. According to published reports, Jay-Z delivered a line cribbed from *The Godfather*: "Lance, you broke my heart,"[20] and then plunged a five-inch blade into Rivera's stomach.[21]

Jay-Z turned himself in for questioning the next day and was released on $50,000 bail. The rapper retained prominent attorney Murray Richman, whose previous clients included fellow hip-hop artist DMX and mobster John Gotti Jr.,[22] and maintained his innocence throughout what turned into nearly two years of legal wrangling. Though Jay-Z faced a lengthy prison term if convicted of felony assault, he ended up pleading guilty to a lesser charge (misdemeanor assault) and received three years of probation as part of the plea agreement. According to the Associated Press and others, Jay-Z told Judge Micki Scherer, "I stabbed Lance Rivera." Rivera also filed a civil suit, which Jay-Z settled by paying him between $500,000 and $1,000,000.[23]

In an interview with Britain's *Sunday Times*, Jay-Z described the incident as "unfortunate" and claimed the media blew the incident out of proportion. "They got hold of the rap-wars thing and ran with it, and that got more egos involved. I knew that situation was not something you play with. It was dangerous, but the sad thing is, it was no different from where I grew up, so I didn't feel threatened. Those battles became like trivial things. For me it was, 'Leave that. Let's get about our business.'"[24]

An extreme devil's advocate might say the whole episode revealed a certain willingness in Jay-Z to take matters into his own hands, to actually attack any threat to his business interests. Such tendencies could come in handy, if harnessed, as an executive. Some even suggested that the whole incident was part of a marketing ploy meant to recreate the mafioso aura of Jay-Z's first album, which features a black-and-white portrait of him as a cigar-puffing, fedora-topped gangster. Employing both Gotti's lawyer and Pacino's line in the Rivera incident served that purpose, and the confluence suggests a person almost cartoonishly infatuated with the image of himself as a mobster. Fortunately for Jay-Z, he shared his underworld idols' ability to beat criminal charges.

On a deeper level, however, the Rivera case echoed earlier experiences in Jay-Z's life. What compelled him to stab Rivera was the same desire for payback that led him to shoot his brother in the shoulder for stealing his jewelry years earlier. To take his career to the next level, to escape the shadow of violence so often unfairly associated with even the most law-abiding members of the hip-hop community, Jay-Z would have to find a balance between street cred and restraint.

As it turned out, whatever pirating Rivera may have done didn't do much to dampen sales of *Life and Times*. The album sold nearly five hundred thousand copies in its first week alone[25] and was certified triple-platinum by the RIAA barely a year later.[26] By that time, Jay-Z, Burke, and Dash were already finding other ways to diversify their burgeoning Roc-A-Fella record label beyond Jay-Z's music.

The first was developing other artists on the label. Usually, this isn't a priority for an independent label—or for the larger parent label. Bernie Resnick, a Philadelphia-based entertainment lawyer who's worked with Jay-Z, explains. "The way it usually works is that when you've got an artist signed to your little independent label, and the major label wants you, then they have to make a deal with the independent label in order to get the rights to the artist. So what they do is they take on the indie on a distribution basis, and they say, 'We'll fund the production of your next album for this artist, and we'll have what they call a first look deal at other artists that you guys sign,' because they really want this artist, the lead artist."[27]

Essentially, the major record label offers a slew of deal-sweeteners to lure a top artist, which is what happened in Jay-Z's deal with Def Jam. Items like the first look deal are usually more of a courtesy than a major part of a deal between an independent label and a major, and perhaps rightfully so: the major label has no way of knowing whether the independent label just got lucky by finding and promoting one artist. Jay-Z's operation was different.

"Roc-A-Fella showed that they were more than just a vehicle to promote the artist Jay-Z," says Resnick. "They also were good at finding and developing and promoting other artists . . . they really kind of expanded their reach and started to reach down into Philadelphia, where there was a sound that was similar stylistically to what they built their business on, and they grabbed a lot of Philly artists and brought them to the New York scene . . . they really became a factory."

Roc-A-Fella discovered, developed, and promoted a host of artists including Philly rappers Beanie Sigel and Freeway, and Brooklyn-born emcee Memphis Bleek (who frequently performs with Jay-Z to this day). To make sure these releases wouldn't fall on deaf ears, Jay-Z appeared on at least one track in each artist's album; his star power helped Sigel's debut sell nearly one million copies. Years later, Roc-A-Fella's own Kanye West would start putting out albums that rivaled Jay-Z's best releases in terms of both sales and critical reception.

Publicity for Roc-A-Fella acts came not only from Jay-Z's appearances on its other artists' songs, but from clever marketing in other arenas. Most record labels dispatched a promotional van for each of their artists, with name, picture, and logo plastered all over the outside. "Inside the van was all the peripherals—posters, stickers, CDs, all that stuff—and it was run by your street team people," explains Serch. "Roc-A-Fella had a Mercedes E-Class 320, white, with the Roc-A-Fella logo on the hood. And that was their promo vehicle. That was a typical Jay maneuver."[28]

Roc-A-Fella Records soon expanded beyond music, thanks to two of Dash's guiding principles: "We shouldn't let other people make money off us, and we shouldn't give free advertising with our lifestyle."[29] Dash wasn't saying that Jay-Z and other Roc-A-Fella artists should stop rapping about designer clothes and high-end liquor; rather, that they should be compensated for the endorsements—or create their own brands. During the late 1990s, Jay-Z and Dash grew fond of Iceberg, an Italian knitwear designer that had recently branched into jeans and sportswear. The Roc-A-Fella crew often showed off their Iceberg gear at glitzy events and dropped its name in a few songs. Largely because of this, Iceberg's sales skyrocketed, at least according to Dash. But when he set up a meeting with the brand's brass to explore some sort of partnership, the response was lukewarm. "The vibe with the company was that they weren't sure they wanted to touch hip-hop. Or have us represent Iceberg," Dash says. "I said: 'Yo, I feel like we've tripled your sales. Help us do our own clothing company, or at least pay us to represent it.' I walked out of there like, I'm definitely doing Rocawear."[30]

Rocawear was the cross-promotional title of the urban clothing line Dash dreamed up shortly thereafter. The venture started with three sewing machines in the back of the Roc-A-Fella Records office; early offerings were limited to T-shirts with the Roc-A-Fella logo stitched on the front. This arrangement posed some problems. "We didn't know how to sew, and we didn't really know people who knew how to sew," says Jay-Z. "We quickly realized that this just wasn't going to work."[31]

So Dash and Jay-Z met with Russell Simmons, founder of Def Jam and Phat Farm clothing, and asked his advice. Simmons put them in touch with industry veterans Alex Bize and Norton Cher; in 1999, Bize and Cher teamed with Dash and Jay-Z to launch Rocawear. The company was soon producing jeans and sweatshirts, eventually launching kids' and plus-size lines as well as footwear and even a cologne, 9IX. Similar to early Roc-A-Fella, Rocawear didn't have the infrastructure to make its own products, so it struck a handful of licensing deals with clothing manufacturers. Within eighteen months of its birth, Rocawear had pulled in $80 million in revenues,[32] something Jay-Z would brag on his 2001 album *The Blueprint*: "One million, two million, three million, four / In 18 months, $80 million more . . . Put me anywhere on God's green Earth, I triple my worth."[33]

Dash encouraged Jay-Z to cross-promote their products whenever he had a chance. If he was going to mention a clothing brand in a song, why give free advertising to someone else when he could boost his own sales with a Rocawear shout-out? Meanwhile, fashionistas who picked up the latest urban styles from Rocawear would, at least in theory, be more likely to buy Jay-Z's music.[34] "Dash is very sharp, very shrewd," says Resnick. "Jay-Z was a talented guy who had a desire to learn business, but wasn't experienced. I think his learning curve was steep but quick. He asked questions and listened to the answers and learned very rapidly."

But cracks began to form in the relationship between the two, starting with the Hard Knock Life tour in 1999. Conceived by Dash, the tour included four dozen cities and united rapper DMX and his Ruff Ryders posse with Jay-Z and Dash's Roc-A-Fella crew. Widely considered the most successful hip-hop tour of its time, it grossed $18 million.[35] Over the months on the road, however, Dash's combative management style began to weigh on Jay-Z and others. One executive called Dash "a defibrillator," meaning he would bluster his way through most situations, the opposite of his generally laid-back counterpart. "Yeah, it's a lot," Jay-Z said of Dash's management style. "But, to his credit, when you have that workin' for you, it's great."[36]

Dash became fixated on Roc-A-Fella films, an obsession that his business partner did not share. Fancying himself a silver-screen auteur, Dash produced *Streets Is Watching*, a straight-to-video flick starring Jay-Z. Released in 1998, the movie was little more than a string of music videos connected by a series of borderline-pornographic interludes. Still, it sold a reported one hundred thousand copies in its first year and netted Roc-A-Fella $2 million.[37] The following year, Dash produced a documentary of the Hard Knock Life tour called *Backstage*, further fueling Dash's Hollywood ambitions. As time wore on, Dash became quick to dismiss Jay-Z's increasingly polished business acumen, even in public. In 2001, he told *The New Yorker*, "If I gotta bring Jay [to a meeting], that mean we got a problem."[38] Even as Dash and Jay-Z's relationship was souring, they teamed with their third partner, Kareem Burke, to launch Armadale Vodka with Scotland's William Grant & Sons. Again, the idea was to stop giving out free advertising and to create another cross-marketing vehicle.

"You always hear us talking about the vodka in one of our songs, so we were like, 'Why are we still making money for everyone else?'" Burke said in a rare interview. "We just acquired the company and said, 'Let's do it ourselves.'" Curiously, few Scots had ever heard of the swill. Shortly after the multimillion-dollar deal was announced, a town councilor in Armadale, Scotland, told U.K.-based publication the *Sun*, "I've never even heard of Armadale Vodka, but these lads must like it a fair bit if they have decided to buy the label."[39]

All the while, Def Jam and parent Universal loomed over Roc-A-Fella. Such relationships were known to follow a certain pattern. "Eventually, when the thing either peters out or is as big as you can get it, then the major label comes in and kind of takes over," says Resnick. "They often have consulting agreements to take in the leaders of that company for a while, but ultimately they're trying to take over the business."

Whether Jay-Z and Dash could agree on the ultimate fate of Roc-A-Fella—or maintain their increasingly strained friendship—was yet to be determined.

3

Building a Notorious Brand

Not long after the last drops of champagne were wiped from the locker room floor, a citywide celebration of the New York Yankees' 2009 World Series victory began. On a brisk November afternoon, I headed down to lower Manhattan along with thousands of New Yorkers who'd called in sick to watch their heroes parade along Broadway. High above the bustle, men in suits pressed their faces to office windows in hopes of catching a glimpse of the players amid the confetti flittering down as the procession headed to its City Hall terminus.

I was there on a hunch that the ceremony would include a surprise appearance by Jay-Z. It was more of an educated guess. The rapper's Big Apple ballad "Empire State of Mind" had become the unofficial anthem of the Yankees as they rolled through the postseason. Throughout the fall, you couldn't turn the radio on for more than fifteen minutes without hearing the song. When Jay-Z performed it at Yankee Stadium just before the first pitch of Game Two, it almost seemed he'd had the venue in mind when he recorded the song months earlier.

After the parade, Mayor Michael Bloomberg presented the players with keys to the city on a dais in front of City Hall and then announced a special guest. Immediately the infectious beat of "Empire" blasted forth from the loudspeakers. A cheer rose above the thumping bass, dwarfing the earlier applause for captain Derek Jeter and World Series MVP Hideki Matsui. Melodic piano notes joined the pop of the bass and Jay-Z strode to the stage.

"Yeah, I'm out that Brooklyn, now I'm down in Tribeca / Right next to De Niro, but I'll be hood forever," thundered Jay-Z as another squall of sound erupted from the spectators. "I'm the new Sinatra, and since I made it here, I can make it anywhere!"

The crowd roared again, swelling against police barriers. People shimmied up streetlights and clambered onto car tops to catch a glimpse of Jay-Z as he began another verse.

"Me, I'm out that Bed-Stuy," he continued. "Home of that boy Biggie . . ."

With that line, Jay-Z connected two important points on a spectrum of powerful associations that have helped him build his own legend. Making himself synonymous with the New York Yankees—the winningest team in the history of professional sports—during the fall of 2009 was simply the latest step. (The following year, he partnered with the team to launch a line of co-branded merchandise, including an official "S. Carter" Yankees jersey.[1]) Jay-Z's first association with a well-known winner came nearly fifteen years earlier in 1994, when, thanks to a series of fortunate events, "that boy Biggie" appeared on Jay-Z's debut album.

At that point in time Christopher Wallace, better known as the Notorious B.I.G., Biggie Smalls, Biggie, or just Big, had ascended to the pinnacle of the rap world with his knack for darkly comical ghetto storytelling. The three-hundred-fifty-pound Brooklyn native delivered rhymes with a melodic huskiness; you could almost hear the cholesterol in his voice when he rapped. His 1994 debut, *Ready to Die*, sold over two million copies in its first year, doubling that figure by the turn of the century. The album featured hits like "Big Poppa" and "Juicy," both of which garner ample radio play to this day; many consider him the greatest rapper of all time.

Biggie employed Clark Kent as his DJ on tour, and this relationship led to Biggie's appearance on Jay-Z's song "Brooklyn's Finest." The spirited duet showed that Jay-Z could hold his own against rap's biggest star, further raising his profile. But the collaboration might not have happened if it weren't for a fortuitous coincidence that occurred at the end of a recording session with Clark Kent and Biggie. Like most producers, Kent carried a bunch of beats around with him on tape at all times; different beats were slated to go to different artists. On this particular occasion, Biggie heard something meant for someone else—and liked it a little too much.

"I forgot to hit the stop button, and instead I hit the forward button, and it went to the next beat, and the next beat was the 'Brooklyn's Finest' beat," recalls Kent. "Big had one boot off, sock halfway off, ran all the way to the back like, 'Is that for me?' And I'm like, 'Nah, it's for Jay.' He said, 'Why you give this mothafucka everything?' . . . I was like, 'Listen, my man's incredible, he's the best. Respectfully, 'cause I know you're a monster. But my man's like the best.'"

Just as he convinced Jay-Z to stop hustling and focus on the music, Kent went to work gently prodding both sides to come together and do the song. Though Jay-Z went to the same high school as Biggie, the two were years apart and didn't really know each other. To further complicate matters, record producer and friend Irv "Gotti" Lorenzo warned Jay-Z that doing a song with Biggie might make Jay-Z seem like a sidekick. "I did not want that record to happen," said Gotti. "I was adamantly against it. I would call Jay every day like, 'No, fuck that! Don't do this record.' I said, 'What I'm scared of is you doin' [a record] with Biggie and you comin' off like his little man. And, nigga, we can't be owning shit if you his little man. You never gon' get that throne.' But [Jay-Z] would call me and be like, 'Nah, but, Gotti, I'm tellin' you, I'm gonna show 'em.'"[2]

So when Kent arrived at the studio and broached the topic of a collaboration, Jay-Z played it cool and Dash remained leery of letting someone else take any of their glory or money, especially Sean "Diddy" Combs, Biggie's close friend and boss at Bad Boy Records. Known in those days as Puffy or Puff, Combs hadn't yet solidified his friendship with Jay-Z and Dash. "[Jay]'s looking at me like, 'I ain't know that guy,'" remembers Kent. "Dame says, 'And, plus, I ain't payin' Puff shit. Fuck Puff.' Those exact words. So I'm like, 'Well, he's my man, I could talk to him.' In my mind, I'm knowing Big wants to be on the beat regardless."

Unbeknownst to Jay-Z and Dash, Biggie was waiting in a car downstairs. After Jay-Z recorded his verse, Kent slipped out to get Biggie. "I'm like, 'Yo, I'm going to the bathroom,'" he recalls. "I go downstairs and I bring Big back up. They're like, 'Oh, you're a funny nigga.' So I'm like, 'That's my man. Big, Jay. Jay, Big. Uh, Dame.'"

With Kent's madcap introduction completed, Jay-Z and Dash consented to the collaboration. Electrified by the challenge, Jay-Z went back into the booth and rerecorded his verses, leaving empty spaces in between for Biggie to record his. "Almost practically to a different song," Kent remembers. "He puts his breaks where they go and he says his verses where they are and the spaces are there. So Big's like, 'I can't fuck with it right now, I need to go home with that.' So he had to take it home to fill in the blanks. And he saw Jay do it without a pen. The funny part is, everybody thinks that Big never wrote his rhymes down. And that wasn't the case. He did, until he saw Jay do that."

Two months later, Biggie met Jay-Z at the studio and

recorded his verses. Afterward, he and Jay-Z walked out of the studio together, leaving Clark Kent to come up with the hook. "They were like, 'Yeah, scratch something,'" recalls Kent. "That's how cavalier things went with the album. When Mary J. Blige sang on the song, it wasn't like, 'Yo, we gotta go get Mary J. Blige.' It was like, 'I know Mary, she sings. Let's give her some money.'"

When "Brooklyn's Finest" started reaching eardrums in 1996, the reactions were exactly what Jay-Z had been hoping for. Rather than defer to the legend, Jay-Z fired back clever rhymes of his own, and the playful sparring between the two elevated the status of both rappers. Listeners saw Jay-Z not as the Scottie Pippen to Biggie's Michael Jordan, but as the Kobe Bryant or the LeBron James—the heir apparent. *Rolling Stone* described the song as "two hungry talents seemingly aware that they had no one to outduel but each other."[3]

The connection proved especially valuable in the late 1990s, when Jay-Z started moving toward a more pop-oriented sound. Where other rappers might have been cast as sellouts, Jay-Z was able to maintain a high level of credibility because of his relationship with the highly respected Biggie. "That's something that burnished his credentials with the underground crowd while he was moving solidly toward trying to do more mainstream work," explains Jeff Chang, the author of *Can't Stop, Won't Stop: A History of the Hip-Hop Generation.* "It was important for him to say, 'Yo, I'm the kid that was on the street just like Big.'"[4]

As much as Jay-Z derived from his relationship with Biggie, Clark Kent believes the latter rapper gained even more.

"It was great for Jay, yes, but in retrospect, it was better for Big," he says. "Because when you hear Big's first album, it was remarkable. But when you hear Big's second album, after he met Jay, it was untouchable. [Jay-Z] made him up the ante."[5]

Flush with the success of their respective classics— Notorious B.I.G.'s *Ready to Die* in 1994 and Jay-Z's *Reasonable Doubt* in 1996—and still riding the success of "Brooklyn's Finest," the pair began discussing plans to start a gangster rap supergroup. The Commission, as it was called, would feature Jay-Z and the Notorious B.I.G. headlining a group that also included Combs, female rapper Charli Baltimore, and a host of others. "The Commission was going to [put out an album] of proportions that no one could fuck with," says Kent. "The lyrical ability on the album was going to be outstanding. That's that. The two best MCs in the game making records together would have been super-dangerous."

The conglomeration would be a counterweight to the West Coast's Death Row, which featured Tupac Shakur, Snoop Dogg, Dr. Dre, and others.

One of the reasons for Biggie's high profile was the vicious enmity between him and former friend Shakur. The conflict started when Shakur was shot five times in the lobby of a New York studio where Biggie and Combs were recording. Believing he'd been set up (though there's never been evidence to support those claims), Shakur responded with vitriolic lyrics that launched arguably the most potent verbal warfare in the history of hip-hop. Thanks in part to his association with Biggie, Jay-Z's name came up more than a few times during the infamous feud. Shakur, who'd first met Jay-Z as a skinny teenager on Big Daddy Kane's tour, even leveled a direct threat in the song "Bomb First": "I'm a Bad Boy killer, Jay-Z die too." But Shakur was gunned down on the Las Vegas strip in 1996; Biggie suffered the same fate on the streets of Los Angeles just months later. Plans for The Commission died with him.

By the time Jay-Z gained mainstream fame in the late 1990s, he had no major adversary, no Tupac to his Biggie, nobody who could raise both his profile and his record sales with a war of words. The only man with potential to fill that role was Queens rapper Nas, whose 1994 album *Illmatic* had placed him among hip-hop royalty. There had been bad blood brewing between the two rappers since 1993, when Nas rebuffed Jay-Z's request to collaborate on a song.[6] When Jay-Z decided to ratchet up his violent rhetoric years later, the conflict exploded into the most heated hip-hop rivalry since Tupac and Biggie's feud.

Jay-Z launched his opening salvo at New York's Summer Jam concert in June 2001 with the song "Takeover." The track was initially a response to insults hurled by Mobb Deep, a Queens-based group with ties to Nas, and featured choice words such as "I don't care if you Mobb Deep, I hold triggers to crews / You little fuck, I got money stacks bigger than you." Jay-Z bragged about selling drugs in the late 1980s while Mobb Deep member Prodigy was attending dance school—and flashed pictures of the rapper as a child wearing a leotard on the arena's JumboTron. With the last line of his verse, he took the challenge directly to his biggest rival: "Ask Nas, he don't want it with [Jay-Z]—no!"[7]

With that, the war was on. "It was no holds barred, the best pound-for-pound emcee battle of all time," says Serch, who served as an executive producer for Nas and helped bring him mainstream recognition in the mid-1990s. After "Takeover" came out, Nas responded with a radio freestyle accusing Jay-Z of being a phony ("the rap version of Sisqó," a one-hit-wonder singer) and calling into question the validity of his drug-dealing claims ("Bore me with your fake coke rhymes / And those times, they never took place, you liar").[8]

Jay-Z fired back in September with the release of his new album, *The Blueprint*, which featured "Takeover" with an extra verse attacking Nas. Choice barbs included "Had a spark when you started but now you're just garbage / Fell from top ten to not mentioned at all" and "Your lame career has come to an end, there's only so long fake thugs can pretend / You ain't live it, you witnessed it from your folks' pad, you scribbled in your notepad and created your life." But the kicker came at the end of the verse, where Jay-Z alluded to an affair he had with Nas's former girlfriend, Carmen Bryan, by saying, "You-know-who did you-know-what with you-know-who / Yeah, just keep that between me and you."[9]

The gauntlet thrown, Nas responded with the devastating track "Ether" on his new album, *Stillmatic*. In the song, Nas called Jay-Z "a fan, a phony, a fake" and accused him of riding Biggie's coattails, asking, "How much of Biggie's rhymes is gonna come out your fat lips?" The song also contained a slew of homophobic lyrics deriding "Gay-Z and Cock-A-Fella Records."[10] The track spurred Jay-Z to follow up with a freestyle radio response focusing on his sexual relationship with Carmen Bryan, spelling out details so salacious that when Jay-Z's own mother heard the recording, she called her son and demanded that he apologize to Nas's family, which he did.

Fueled by the feud, Jay-Z's music was selling faster than ever; his new album achieved platinum status barely a month after its release. "What really became interesting about that battle is how Jay used it to create more popularity for his music and less popularity for the battle, and I think it was a very smart business move on Jay's part," says Serch. "Jay used that opportunity to just put out great record after great record, and got with some of the hottest producers, and knew that every DJ in the country was spinning his records, and used that to propel everything he had in his catalog at the time."

In his duel with Nas, Jay-Z had managed to create a microcosm of the West Coast–East Coast drama of the previous decade. But this war was between rappers on different sides of the same city, and, more important, it never escalated into the sort of violence that the Tupac-Biggie battle did. Whether that was an indication that Jay-Z simply fanned the feud's flames to sell more records or just an acknowledgment that he and Nas were more restrained in their dealings is uncertain. Chang believes Jay-Z engineered the clash to keep himself relevant on the street and to satisfy the hardcore fan base that he risked alienating with some of the more poppy songs he'd been putting out around that time.

"You [can] read it as him trying to take care of the core audience," says Chang. "[Jay-Z and Nas] are sort of battling for the crown that Biggie left behind. There's all the imagery that's sitting there waiting for a journalist to sculpt it into the new battle royale, and for everybody to make money off of that. It extended both of their careers quite a bit."[11]

In 2005, after the conflict had cooled, Jay-Z announced a handful of upcoming live shows with the ominous moniker "I Declare War." It seemed that Jay-Z was poised to reignite his battle with Nas. His first show in the series took place at New Jersey's Continental Airlines Arena and contained all the trappings of a military declaration. The stage was laid out to look like the Oval Office, complete with presidential seal and red phone. Two hours into the show, Jay-Z was in the midst of a song from his second album called "Where I'm From." He delivered the line "I'm from where niggas pull your card / And argue all day about who's the best MC: Biggie, Jay-Z, or Nas," and then the music stopped abruptly.

"This was called I Declare War," Jay-Z said, addressing the audience. "It's bigger than I declare war. It's like the motherfuckin' president presents the United Nations. So you know what I did for hip-hop? I said, 'Fuck that shit.' Let's go, [Nas]!" With that, a man in a military jacket hopped onto the stage, none other than Jay-Z's archrival. The two stars unleashed a furious rendition of Jay-Z's song "Dead Presidents," which samples one of Nas's songs, then shook hands in front of the ecstatic crowd.[12]

"People can't tell you where they were when their kid was born," says Serch. "But they could tell you where they were when Nas hit that stage. That was a historic moment in hip-hop. Because no other hip-hop battle ended amicably while both artists were still on top."

Ever the trendsetter, Jay-Z was able to bring about reconciliation between two warring camps, something that had never been done on that scale in rap. Just as conflict sold records in the old days, Jay-Z believed that high-profile peacemaking was the way of the future. His plan to monetize it would be revealed later; in the meantime, he merely hinted at it as he stood with Nas in front of twenty thousand screaming fans.

"This," said Nas, "is hip-hop history."

"All that beef shit is wack," Jay-Z shouted. "Let's get this money."[13]

Signaled by the resolution of his battle with Nas, Jay-Z's career was entering a new phase. This was a period that would be characterized not by spats, coastal or local, but by placing himself, both lyrically and physically, in the presence of people associated with victory. Jay-Z's early muses included John Gotti and Michael Corleone; by 2003, Jay-Z was calling himself "the black Warren Buffett." Jay-Z gave himself the nicknames Jay-Hova, Hova, and Hov, all derived from the godly name Jehovah. There was no doubt he aimed to cement his status as hip-hop's ultimate deity.

In that vein, Jay-Z also likened himself to another god of sorts: Michael Jordan. Whether bragging that he was "the Mike Jordan of recordin'" or saying, "I'm Michael Jordan, I play for the team I own," Jay-Z drew a number of parallels to His Airness. And what better company to keep—with five MVP trophies and six championship rings (not to mention plenty of his own business acumen), Jordan is considered the greatest basketball player of all time. "[Jay] spent a lot [of] time in his career comparing himself to Michael Jordan, and not for no reason," says Touré. "That's what he thinks of himself as."[14]

Jordan was born in Brooklyn and smoothed out his style of play over the course of his career in a way that was similar to the evolution of Jay-Z's rap—at least according to Jay-Z. "In his early days, Jordan was rocking a cradle, cranking it, all crazy, but he wasn't winning championships," Jay-Z once explained to *The New Yorker.* "And then, later in his career, he just had a fadeaway jump shot, and they won six titles. Which was the better Jordan? I don't know."[15]

The two would prove to have even more in common beyond 2003, from retiring and un-retiring to leaving their original careers with the aim of becoming serious businessmen. But in the summer of 2003, as Jay-Z's fame reached new heights, he would make the most Jordanesque gesture of his career.

4

Jay-Z's First Basketball Team

Over lunch on a damp autumn day in Harlem, hip-hop pioneer Fred "Fab 5 Freddy" Brathwaite seems mired in an internal debate. He's deciding whether to tell me something about Jay-Z.

We've spent the past twenty minutes cheerfully swapping generalities, but when I ask for specifics, the pauses grow longer, his brow becomes furrowed.

"Can you tell me some kind of anecdote that shows how Jay-Z thinks?" I press. "Any moment that stands out in your mind?"

"Let me think," he says, munching his Caesar salad.

"So . . ." I continue, stalling. "I'm trying to, you know, get . . . inside his brain."

Silence.

"I like the way they hooked this salad up," he mutters.

Then he blinks a long blink, as though clenching his eyelids longer will dull the regret of whatever he's about to tell me. He opens his eyes.

"I believe it was the summer of 2003 . . ."

The scene was Holcombe Rucker Playground, a hallowed slab of asphalt wedged between the Harlem River and Frederick Douglass Boulevard in upper Manhattan. Jay-Z's task: to assemble a team to play and win the Entertainers Basketball Classic (EBC), a tournament that offered no prize money, no gilded trophy—just victory, a muse if ever Jay-Z had one. "Where are you victory?" he asks in one song. "I need you desperately—not just for the moment, but to make history."[1]

Harlem schoolteacher Holcombe Rucker first staged a tournament at the courts in 1946 with the goal of keeping local teenagers out of mischief.[2] Within a few years, New York's finest players were flocking to "the Rucker" to hone their skills every summer. Legends like Wilt Chamberlain and Julius Erving would later grace its courts alongside the city's best street ballers. The courts at 155th Street became a node of cultural diffusion for the thousands of people who came to watch the games every summer, a place where the newest street fashions were unfurled, evaluated, and propagated.

Hip-hop emissaries like Fab 5 Freddy have long taken cues from what they see at the Rucker—the clothes worn by fashionable spectators, the moves made by neighborhood break-dancers, the music blasting from boom boxes in the stands, and even the tricks performed by the players on the court. Fab calls it "the place where street life and hustlers and sports intersect."[3] In the 1970s and 1980s, local drug lords would sponsor and organize teams to play in the summer tournament, always trying to lure an NBA basketball player or two to headline their squad. When the authorities cracked down on the illicit trade in the early 1990s, profits waned and hip-hop artists took over the managerial role.

The EBC offered a perfect opportunity for Jay-Z to create a muscular cross-marketing engine for S. Carter, his namesake Reebok sneaker; the 40/40 Club, his new nightspot; and *The Black Album*, due out in the fall of 2003, which he claimed would be his last before ending his recording career and focusing on his business ventures. To tie everything together, he had a splashy publicity vehicle in mind: the silver screen. His first ventures into film had been overseen by Dash, but by the summer of 2003, the pair's relationship was on the rocks. The prior year, while Jay-Z was vacationing on a yacht in the Mediterranean, Dash fired a handful of Roc-A-Fella employees and elevated rapper and longtime friend Cameron "Cam'ron" Giles to vice president status, all without consulting his partner. Jay-Z returned a few days later and vetoed the move, causing a public rift with Cam'ron and tension with Dash.[4] Rumors of a permanent split between the two Roc-A-Fella founders had swirled ever since.

So Jay-Z selected Fab, not Dash, for his latest film project. "Jay reached out to me with an idea to do a commercial for this Reebok sneaker," says Fab. "He also wanted me to do a documentary on his basketball team." The plan was to capture every moment of what promised to be a victorious romp through the summer tournament and eventually turn it into a feature-length documentary about the time Jay-Z conquered the Rucker.

Fab was an ideal auteur for the project. A dapper urban tastemaker himself, he had helped export hip-hop music and style from the fire-scorched streets of the South Bronx to the primordial post-funk milieu of Greenwich Village in the early 1980s. By turning the eyes of downtown collectors and gallery owners toward graffiti, he helped establish the art form, and hip-hop music soon followed across the river to Manhattan. Fab would go on to host the hit show *Yo! MTV Raps* in the 1990s; in the new millennium, he developed a professional relationship with Jay-Z.

By 2003, Jay-Z was perfectly situated to gather an all-world street basketball team. Coming off his sixth platinum studio album in six years, he'd attained some measure of hip-hop immortality and vaulted into the pantheon of mainstream pop culture with radio-friendly jams like "Big Pimpin'" and "Hard Knock Life (Ghetto Anthem)." The triumphal ballads of Jay-Z and his Roc-A-Fella cohorts blared from countless automobile sound systems while millions donned clothing from his Rocawear line.

Reebok released Jay-Z's S. Carter sneaker that April. Each pair was packaged in a box that included a CD with sneak-peek samples from Jay-Z's *Black Album*, due out the following fall. The first ten thousand pairs of the $150 shoe flew off shelves within an hour of release, making it Reebok's fastest-selling shoe of all time.[5] The following month, Jay-Z opened the 40/40 Club with partners Desirée Gonzalez and Juan Perez in Manhattan's Flatiron district. The nightspot's name played on the term used to describe the tiny group of baseball players who have stolen forty bases and clubbed forty home runs in the same season, aiming to lend the club a sense of exclusivity. From its inception, promoters billed the dim, high-ceilinged lounge as a place where stargazers might catch a glimpse of their favorite athlete or musician. Decades earlier, Joe Namath and Billy Joel could be found celebrating their victories uptown at Elaine's; now, the likes of Derek Jeter and Jay-Z would frequent the 40/40.

To maximize his cross-marketing opportunities, Jay-Z arranged to have a bus plastered with images of his sneaker. Before each game at the Rucker, the players would meet in midtown and clamber aboard. They'd make the thirty-minute drive up to Harlem and stride into the Rucker to the screams of thousands of adoring fans. After decimating the opposition, they'd hop in the bus and head back downtown to celebrate at the 40/40 Club, a real-time sound track of Jay-Z's songs thumping all the while. "I was really impressed with him bringing all these things together, really cool street stuff and this whole business thing," says Fab. "That sneaker was selling, and the whole excitement around that tournament was giving credence to the shoe."

Synergies aside, the EBC wasn't simply a marketing whim.

Jay-Z, a lifelong basketball fan, intended to win the summer tournament. To accomplish this goal, he'd have to unseat the defending champions, rival rapper Fat Joe's Terror Squad—a team that boasted rugged NBA players Stephon Marbury and Ron Artest, both of whom had honed their skills in New York school yards. Jay-Z was unfazed. "He was like, 'I'm going to bring this team together . . . I'm only going to do it once, and obviously I plan to win,'" recalls Fab. "Then *The Black Album* was supposed to come out, and then he was going to retire."

As summer settled over New York, Fab began filming and Jay-Z went to work as general manager. Previous Rucker squads were packed with street ballers, and only the best boasted one or two NBA players. Jay-Z had something different in mind. He recruited two Rucker veterans, rebound machine John "Franchise" Strickland and sweet shooter Reggie "Hi-5" Freeman, and then set about rounding out his squad with NBA players, finally accumulating a list of hard-court warriors that was almost Homeric in scope. There was power forward Kenyon Martin, the first pick of the NBA Draft three years earlier; Los Angeles swingman Lamar Odom, a well-rounded player now better known for his marriage to Khloe Kardashian; and Tracy McGrady, a lanky twenty-three-year-old who had averaged 32.1 points per game during the 2003–2004 season, tops in the NBA.

Amazingly enough, McGrady wasn't even the most famous player who agreed to play on Jay-Z's team. That honor belonged to a teenager who'd just scored a $90 million endorsement deal with Nike[6] months before playing his first NBA game: LeBron James, the top pick in the NBA draft and the heir apparent to Michael Jordan's best-player-in-the-world mantle. Though James wasn't going to play for Jay-Z's squad before agreeing to terms on a contract with the Cleveland Cavaliers—an event that a street-ball injury could jeopardize—his mere presence on the sidelines at the Rucker contributed to the growing frenzy surrounding Team S. Carter.

Hours after the last revelers staggered out into the muggy Manhattan morning following the June 18 grand opening of Jay-Z's 40/40 Club, Rucker Park was set to host the opening game of the EBC. But a steady drizzle forced the game from the Rucker to a backup location, a gym called Gauchos in the Bronx. Most of Jay-Z's NBA recruits hadn't yet joined the team, and with only a smattering of pros (including the 6' 10" Odom, who served as a primary ball handler in the opener), Jay-Z's squad suffered an embarrassing loss.

"Lamar Odom, who's from Queens, he got clowned that game," recalls Fab. "He tried to do one of them classic Rucker trick maneuvers where he tried to do something crazy with the ball, and the kid snatched it . . . On the bus coming back, they all huddled and said, 'We've got to get a point guard!'" Jay-Z, his partner Perez, and Mike Kyser, another member of Jay-Z's inner circle, put their heads together. One of the more intriguing names that emerged was Sebastian Telfair. Jay-Z first met the Brooklyn high school star two years earlier when the two sat together by chance at a St. John's

University game. "He asked who I was," recalls Telfair. "I told him I'm Sebastian Telfair, one of the top players in the country. He said, 'Oh yeah?' And he typed my name into his Motorola."[7]

Jay-Z and his brain trust discovered that pro teams were already salivating at the possibility of Telfair making the jump from high school to the NBA. He had it all—the name, rolling off the tongue with the sort of phonetic deliciousness reserved for Dickens characters; the story, a golden child rising from the hardscrabble housing projects on Coney Island; the lineage, as a cousin of Stephon Marbury; and the moves, including a wicked crossover and no-look passes delivered so convincingly that they sometimes bounced off the chests of unsuspecting teammates.

On the day of Team S. Carter's second game, Telfair found himself in the 40/40 Club, awaiting an audience with Jay-Z and Perez. Standing just shy of six feet and about one hundred sixty pounds soaking wet, the baby-faced teenager didn't look the part of an all-world street-ball team savior. "When I walked in, they were like, 'Aw, he's a kid, how's he going to help us?'" recalls Telfair. "I looked at Jay and I said, 'I'm from *Brooklyn*.' And he just started laughing. But by the end of that night, he knew what exactly I meant when I said, 'I'm from Brooklyn.'"

Telfair would showcase skills honed on the Coney Island asphalt, but not before learning a kind of showmanship he hadn't picked up on the Brooklyn basketball courts. That evening, he boarded the S. Carter bus to find Sean Combs and Beyoncé Knowles, by then Jay-Z's girlfriend, casually eating soul food alongside a half-dozen NBA stars. The bus rumbled up to Rucker Park. When the dazed Telfair started to disembark, Jay-Z motioned him back. "Come here, come here," the mogul said, smiling. "You've got to make a grand entrance." So they paused for a moment and waited as the gathering flock of fans noticed the bus. Then Jay-Z took LeBron James and Telfair by the arm and strolled out into the warm Harlem evening to a thunderous greeting, the crowd parting in front of them.

"Anything that Jay was doing," recalls Telfair, "he was going to do it in a way that it hadn't been done before, in a way that people would talk about it." The young point guard took that lesson to heart, dazzling the Rucker crowd with an array of tricky no-look passes, devastating crossovers, and delectable finger rolls. Telfair racked up twenty-five points and Team S. Carter rolled to its first victory.

Still, the opening game loss haunted Jay-Z, and that was apparent even to his seventeen-year-old point guard. "He hates to lose," says Telfair. Or, as Jay-Z himself says in one song, "I will not lose, ever."[8] Losing as Brathwaite's film cameras rolled was the worst of all. So Jay-Z went to work once again, using his gravitational pull to lure additional reinforcements. One of the first calls went to Jamal Crawford, a talented guard who met Jay-Z through Michael Jordan in 2001 while playing for the Bulls. "Jay called me on the phone and told me that he needed me to come down," Crawford remembers. "The one thing Jay said on the phone was, 'We can't lose.'"[9]

The way Crawford described it, Jay-Z wasn't saying that losing was impossible—rather, that it was *too* possible, an unthinkable outcome etched into his mind by the opening night loss. He'd entered the EBC to create the best team the tournament had seen, to supercharge his legacy, and to win. That was the only acceptable result. (In his song "History," he raps, "Rank me among the greats, either one, two, or three / If I ain't number one, then I failed you, victory."[10]) Fortunately, his star power proved contagious. Not only did Crawford happily agree to join the team and fly to New York for the weekly games, the Chicago standout recruited seven-foot teammate Eddy Curry to join as well.

Crawford remembers being uncharacteristically tense the first time he stepped onto the court at the Rucker. "I was so, so nervous. It's different than the NBA," he says. "The fans are right there on you. It's just unbelievable, the atmosphere, you can't duplicate it anywhere." But Crawford soon shook off his jitters. With the two Bulls in Jay-Z's stable, Team S. Carter launched into a winning streak that would take them to the brink of a street ball championship.

On overcast summer evenings in New York, twilight gives way to cloud cover that reflects the pinky-orange glow of a hundred thousand streetlamps back at the avenues of the city below. Sidewalks slowly release the heat collected during the day, leaving a soupy shroud of asphalt-smelling warmth just above the street.

The summer of 2003 was packed with those sorts of nights. Electric fans throbbed vainly in open windows above the Rucker as Team S. Carter barreled through the tournament. Courtside bleachers swelled with fans hoping to see a nasty no-look pass by Telfair, a backboard-bending dunk from Crawford, or, even better, a glimpse of Jay-Z himself. With the stands packed, some spectators even shimmied into trees overlooking the court to watch, all while Brathwaite's cameras rolled. As the incredible run wore on, the mere sight of the star-packed S. Carter bus was known to cause minor riots wherever it went. Fab recalls the frenzy. "You've got the S. Carter bus, and everybody was like, 'Aaah!' because everybody knew about Jay-Z and the sneaker, and then we'd roll up to the Rucker and everybody'd be like, 'Aaaah!'" he says. "There was so much excitement."

Jay-Z grew close to many of the players on his team, especially James and Crawford, who eventually became a part of the rapper's S. Carter Academy, a Reebok-sponsored cadre of athletes. Members appeared in television commercials with Jay-Z, and although the academy is now defunct, many of the athletes still flash the trademark "Roc" sign—their hands connecting at thumb and forefinger to form a diamond shape—on national television after making spectacular plays.

In addition to making sure everyone on his team received VIP treatment at the 40/40 Club, Jay-Z invited the players to watch him record tracks for his new album at nearby Bassline Recording Studio. Like other observers before him, Crawford was impressed the first time he saw Jay-Z lay down vocals in the recording booth. "The beat came on and he just kind of went mumbling to himself for a while, no pen, no paper, no nothing," says Crawford. "Then he goes in the booth and does the whole verse, and everybody in the whole studio is hearing the verse at the same time, so we were all just blown away. He didn't stutter, didn't make any mistakes."

Even while recording an album and jetting around the country to coheadline the Rock the Mic tour a few days per week with 50 Cent, the thirty-three-year-old Jay-Z remained extremely focused on details, a trait surprising for a boss of his stature—and one that would serve him well during his tenure as president of Def Jam starting in 2005. As general manager of Team S. Carter, he'd contact players personally to make sure they were coming to games, even arranging transportation. "He'd call you, he'd e-mail you," recalls Telfair. "If I couldn't get all the way out there, he'd make sure to have a car come pick me up."

Above all, Telfair marveled at how much time Jay-Z put into the team. "He didn't get any money for this, this was just fun for him," says Telfair. "I can just imagine how serious he is about something that's making millions and millions of dollars." To be fair, Jay-Z was being compensated in a way that could only be measured in the number of heads-turned-per-trip as the S. Carter bus cruised from Midtown to Harlem, or crowd-volume-per-point-scored by his team at the Rucker.

There was also the marketing component. Fab was impressed by the way Jay-Z was able to go into an edgy tastemaker's mecca like the Rucker, blatantly promote a shoe made by a major corporation for mass consumption, and not be cast as a sellout. Perhaps because of his vivid lyrics and gritty past, he was able to avoid the corporate stigma while promoting his product in tandem with his team at the Rucker. Jay-Z was a sellout in a more favorable way: Reebok sold all five hundred thousand units in the first run of the S. Carter shoe that summer.[11]

"It was just a real synergistic way of taking the things he does, how he lives, making it really big, and still 'keeping it real' in the almost cliché urban sense," says Fab. "It was a point where his business acumen was beginning to move to this other level because that whole summer, I didn't see Damon Dash around at all. So it was kind of obvious that something might be happening between them."

Putting together a team of NBA all-stars, renting a tour bus, and hiring Fab to film the whole enterprise was a calculated risk. A tournament victory would bring Jay-Z further street cred, more marketing clout with the consumers to whom he was marketing his shoes, and a victorious feature-length documentary from Fab. Team S. Carter clinched a championship showdown with Fat Joe's Terror Squad by early August. With a roster that included Crawford, McGrady, and James, victory seemed all but guaranteed.

Brathwaite noticed Jay-Z's penchant for shrewd risk-reward analysis even when the rapper was relaxing. He and a few of the athletes sometimes passed the time on the bus by playing a poker cousin called Guts, which is characterized by frequent showdowns and fast-multiplying pots. "I don't play poker, but Guts is a game that Jay talked about a lot on the bus," says Fab. "I think there's a connection between that and business. It's all a gamble. And I guess the thing that makes one gambler better than the next is those that understand when they have a better chance to win."

Around this time, Fab's monologue is interrupted by the trill of his iPhone. He thumbs the screen and draws it to his ear.

"Yo," he says. "Listen, I'm doing a little interview right now. I'ma hit you when I finish with my man, all right?"

He puts the phone down. I'm beginning to wonder if he's still planning to tell me whatever it was that caused his apparent anxiety earlier.

"Want some fries?" I inquire.

"No, I'm good, no thanks."

"So what happened in the end with the basketball team? Who won?"

"Oh, god, that's a whole . . . oh, man," he says, shaking his head. There's a pregnant pause and another long blink.

"Well, here's how it went," he continues slowly. "And maybe from this you can cull some interesting tidbit about the way Jay does what he does. We played through this tournament, and it was so exciting. And guess what happens for the final: it's going to be the S. Carter Jay-Z team versus Fat Joe's Terror Squad. The day has arrived . . ."

As the morning of August 14 faded into the afternoon, the mercury climbed into the mid-90s, promising another heavy New York night at the Rucker for the final game of the season. Jay-Z had guided his team to the precipice of victory after a summer of scheming, schmoozing, cross-marketing, and testing his skills as a manager.

A few hours before the game, Fab met up with Jay-Z to prepare in the air-conditioned cool of the studio, as usual. "But this day it was special," remembers Fab. "Because now LeBron was going to play . . . and Shaquille O'Neal was in New York in a hotel as a secret weapon that was going to be brought into the park solo to play for us."

"And while I'm up in the studio, I have my guy plugging in some lights, he was going to interview one of the players, and all the lights go out in the studio. I go, 'What happened?' Then I hear some people upstairs saying there's no lights. I'm like, 'What's going on in the building?'"

The disturbance wasn't unique to the studio. High electrical demand had forced a power plant near Cleveland offline, straining high-voltage rural power lines into a failure that cascaded across the entire electrical grid. The ensuing blackout left some fifty-five million citizens in the United States and Canada without electricity for nearly twenty-four hours. As traffic lights shut down, gridlock engulfed Manhattan. A deluge of wireless activity briefly rendered cell phones useless. Crawford and Curry were stuck in their hotel rooms. Fab and Jay-Z were stranded downtown, and the other players were scattered across the city. Telfair, who'd shown up early at the Rucker, had to walk home across the Brooklyn Bridge. Without electricity, there was no way to light the nighttime asphalt at the storied courts.

"It was havoc. There was confusion," says Fab. "Bottom line, no game."

The tournament's organizers rescheduled the game for the following week. But there was a major problem: Jay-Z had already booked a private jet for the next day, August 15, to whisk him and Beyoncé away for a two-week vacation to Europe, one of their first vacations together. They had to be back in New York for the MTV Video Music Awards on August 28 at Radio City Music Hall, where a slew of Beyoncé's videos were up for awards—including "Crazy in Love," featuring Jay-Z. Postponing their departure by a week would cut their vacation from two weeks to four or five days, and with Beyoncé set to start her first solo tour in the fall, there was no time to reschedule. Committed though he was to his basketball team, Jay-Z refused to cancel the trip and risk alienating his superstar girlfriend in what was still an early stage of their relationship.

So when Fab showed up at the Rucker to document the final game the following week without Jay-Z, there was total chaos. "The team showed up but none of the ringers, because it's only Jay that can make those calls and put those guys on flights," he says. "There was a whole confrontation between the manager, the team, and the park guys . . . they decide that the game has been forfeited, and by default Fat

Joe wins." When Jay-Z returned from Europe, he told Fab to stop working on the film. The project was dead.

"Jay-Z didn't want to put it out. I didn't want to, you know . . ." says Fab, trailing off. "It's one of those interesting stories." Fab's tapes contain hours upon hours of footage, from candid interactions between Jay-Z and his players to shots of some of the best basketball ever to grace the Rucker. Yet they remain filed away, destined to fall short of the big screen. "Who knows? It could have run the festivals," says Fab. "That was the pinnacle of the Rucker, in that period. It got so big, and that was kind of the crescendo tournament."

So, after a whole summer of meticulously organizing one of the best teams ever to set foot at New York's most famous court this side of Madison Square Garden, why would Jay-Z scuttle the documentary that was going to put it all together? The answer is simple: he didn't win. Jay-Z said all along that he was only going to do the tournament once, and that he was going to win. And though the final game was never played, the final game was never won, either. He felt that publicizing anything less than victory would somehow taint his legacy despite the other victories notched that summer— buzz, marketing, sneaker sales, and a stronger relationship with his future wife.

He still managed to achieve those goals, even without scoring an official victory in the tournament; what he did win was much more important than what he didn't win. These days, when people talk about the summer of 2003 at Rucker Park, they don't remember that Team S. Carter forfeited the championship game. All they remember is a golden moment on the hallowed blacktop. "Everywhere I go, people still talk about it," says Telfair. "It was a unique time for Rucker basketball. It's always going to have hype, but it will never be done how Jay-Z did it."

It's safe to say that there aren't many who dwell on which team actually won the tournament. Except for maybe Jay-Z.

Early Retirement

The date is November 25, 2003; the place, Madison Square Garden. The lights have just gone out, and a sellout crowd hums with anticipation. It might be the biggest retirement party in the history of retirement parties. Some twenty thousand spectators, including entertainers Sean Combs, Usher Raymond, Beyoncé Knowles, Kanye West, and Mary J. Blige, are here to celebrate thirty-three-year-old Jay-Z and the ostensible conclusion of his illustrious recording career.

A single spotlight shines down from the rafters, revealing celebrity announcer Michael Buffer. Boxing bells clang the air clear. "L-l-ladies and gentlemen," Buffer rumbles. "Tonight we've come to Madison Square Garden, New York City, to see and hear a legendary superstar."

"Uh-uh-uh," grunts Jay-Z from a microphone offstage, bumping the buzzing crowd up a few more decibels.

"From Marcy projects, Bed-Stuy, Brooklyn, New York," Buffer booms, "presenting the one, the only, undisputed, undefeated heavyweight champion of the world of hip-hop, he is . . . JAY-Z!"

The lights flash on, the bass thumps out the beat for Jay-Z's "What More Can I Say," and the main man saunters to the stage amid a swirl of white smoke. The stands tremble as he delivers his first line: "Never been a nigga this good for this long / This hood or this pop, this hot, or this strong!"[1]

The crowd roars its agreement. Later in the evening, Jay-Z rhymes the motives behind his retirement to the thousands of adorers still undulating to his every word: "Jay's status appears to be at an all-time high / Perfect time to say good-bye."[2]

It might be hard to believe that, just a few weeks shy of his thirty-fourth birthday, Jay-Z decided to call an end to his hip-hop recording career. But as he himself put it, he was already the Michael Jordan of hip-hop. Jordan retired for the first time at age thirty after doing everything there was to be done in basketball: specifically, winning three championships and three MVP awards in his first nine years. Jay-Z did hip-hop's equivalent by notching seven platinum albums and a Grammy award in his first eight. In case he ever got the itch to rap again, Jay-Z reserved the right to "come back like Jordan" in a song on *The Black Album*.[3]

The album featured production by some of the brightest

stars in hip-hop, including Timbaland, the Neptunes, and Jay-Z protégé Kanye West. Absent were most of the producers who had churned out the strongest beats of Jay-Z's early career—namely DJ Clark Kent, DJ Ski, and DJ Premier. The latter had planned to contribute a track, but Jay-Z wanted to release *The Black Album* on Black Friday, and this caused an unworkable scheduling conflict for Premier.[4] Even so, when the album hit stores two weeks early in response to a leak, few critics complained about the absence of *Reasonable Doubt*'s wizened beat makers. "Old-school and utterly modern, it showed Jay at the top of his game," declared *Rolling Stone*. "[He was] able to reinvent himself as a rap classicist at the right time, as if to cement his place in hip-hop's legacy for generations to come."[5] Jay-Z's supposed swan song earned a Grammy nomination for Best Rap Album, and his song "99 Problems" won a Grammy for Best Solo Rap Performance.

Jay-Z also authorized the release of an a cappella version of his album, thus encouraging scads of remixes—most notably *The Grey Album*, producer Brian "Danger Mouse" Burton's mash-up of Jay-Z's *Black Album* and the Beatles' *White Album*. The record clocked one hundred thousand digital downloads in a matter of days after EMI, which owns certain rights to the Beatles' recordings, filed a cease and desist order.[6] The publicity generated by *The Grey Album* and other mash-ups further publicized *The Black Album*, which went on to sell over three million copies.[7] Though Jay-Z's retirement would last only three years, many believed he was serious in 2003 when he said the album would be his final solo effort.

"I think he thought so at the time," says Ahmir "Questlove" Thompson, the drummer of the hip-hop ensemble the Roots, which backed Jay-Z at the Madison Square Garden concert. "And that maybe it was best to get out while he was ahead."[8]

Jay-Z was indeed ahead. But by November 2003, he had grown tired of hip-hop. He'd been struck, he claimed, by a sense of ennui, and left bored by a lack of competition. In his opinion, there wasn't a Magic Johnson or a Larry Bird, or even a Charles Barkley, to his Jordan. "It's not like it was with Big and Pac, hip-hop's corny now," he declared in 2003. "I love when someone makes a hot album and then you've got to make a hot album. I love that. But [hip-hop] ain't hot."[9] Though he dabbled in different genres in the wake of his retirement from hip-hop, releasing platinum-selling collaborations with R&B singer R. Kelly and rock group Linkin Park, Jay-Z's main motive for retirement was business. He wanted to shift from the music side to the management side of the recording industry, and as his rap career progressed, he sprinkled clues of this ambition throughout his oeuvre.

Jay-Z's early music videos portrayed the grit and grime of his Brooklyn upbringing and subsequent years as a hustler, taking MTV audiences from the comfort of their couches to the seedy motels he frequented as a drug runner in his adolescence. By 1998, Jay-Z seemed more concerned with impressing his audience with a preponderance of costly champagnes, tropical vacation locations, and women in bikinis. Within a few years, though, a more refined vision of success emerged—party atmosphere, yes, but something more befitting a billionaire oil tycoon than a successful drug dealer.

Jay-Z's video for "Excuse Me Miss," a song released shortly before his retirement, gives a clue to the shift in his priorities. The video opens with the rapper sitting in a leather armchair, puffing a Zino Platinum cigar. He then advises viewers on appropriate champagne pairings for the video, as if it were a foie gras appetizer in need of a liquid complement. "You can't even drink Cristal on this one," he says with a wave of his cigar. "You've got to drink Cris-TAHL."[10] (At about $40 per cigar, Zino is among the world's most expensive; Steve Stoute, a frequent Jay-Z business partner, helped launch the brand and holds a large equity stake.[11])

The rest of the video shows Jay-Z in a pin-striped suit, catching the eye of an elegant woman in a chic nightclub. Between descriptions of his Maybach land yacht waiting outside and prominent product placement of Roc-A-Fella's Armadale Vodka, Jay-Z envisions the evolution of their relationship. He imagines text messaging the lucky lady from his BlackBerry while solving a corporate squabble late at night in a boardroom filled with dark-suited men; later, he pictures himself and his hypothetical girlfriend disembarking from a private jet onto a tarmac loaded with seven luxury cars, each adorned with a vanity plate bearing a different day of the week. At one point in the song, Jay-Z delivers the line "You know what I'm sitting on," leading the audience to expect another vehicular boast, but instead mentions one of his business ventures. Though the song contains more high-end automobile advertisements than the latest issue of *Robb Report*, it's clear that Jay-Z's desire to be seen as a legitimate businessman trumps his need to be seen as a big spender, though the former certainly doesn't cancel the latter. Still, for a rap video, the shift from simply flaunting wealth to flaunting wealth *and* explaining how it might be generated is an unusual—if not revolutionary—departure.

The shift was also a function of Jay-Z wanting to keep his art true to his life. "I think the problem with people, as they start to mature, they say, 'Rap is a young man's game,' and they keep trying to make young songs," Jay-Z said in a 2010 interview. "I don't want to stop listening to hip-hop when I'm fifty years old. But I don't want to listen to something I can't relate to. I can't relate to a guy in a big mansion telling me he's going to shoot me."[12]

Much as Jay-Z gave up the lucrative life of drug dealing so that he could focus on music, he gave up the young man's game of rap to become a full-time businessman. The ventures that lured him away from the microphone were not limited to his existing portfolio of Rocawear, Roc-A-Fella Records, and the 40/40 Club, but included the possibility of other options down the line—namely, an executive position at a major record label.

At Roc-A-Fella parent Def Jam, its parent Island Def Jam— and at Universal, the corporate parent of both—members of upper management had long flirted with the idea of offering

Jay-Z an executive post. As time went on, he became more and more infatuated with the idea, going out of his way to curry favor with those who might be able to help him land such a position down the line.

During a European vacation with Beyoncé in the summer of 2003—the trip he took instead of attending the rescheduled final game of the EBC—Jay-Z stopped in the south of France to meet with U2 front man Bono and Interscope Records CEO Jimmy Iovine. He left a strong impression on both. "He's a talent, he's a talent finder, he's a record maker, he's a magnet, he's creative, he's smart, he sees the music business as a 360 degrees [business] rather than just linear, he's the modern record guy," Iovine said in a 2005 interview. "He's got great feel, he's got great taste, and he knows how to market things. The rest you can learn."[13]

Months before his Madison Square Garden retirement concert in the fall of 2003, Jay-Z started having conceptual conversations with Doug Morris, Universal's CEO, about joining the company's management ranks. "I liked him because he comes from an entrepreneurial background," Morris said two years later. "When you run a label you learn the whole thing, you get the broad idea of what this business is all about."[14]

Jay-Z got his chance in 2004, thanks to a complicated game of executive musical chairs set off by Seagram scion Edgar Bronfman Jr., chief of Warner Music Group, one of the industry's four major record companies. Bronfman lured Lyor Cohen, a longtime Jay-Z mentor and president of Island

Def Jam, to run Warner. Morris then filled the gap left by Cohen by hiring Antonio "L.A." Reid, another Jay-Z admirer. Reid clashed with incumbent Def Jam president Kevin Liles, who then followed Cohen to Warner, leaving the Def Jam presidency vacant. Reid and Def Jam pounced, offering Jay-Z a lucrative three-year deal to become the label's president.[15]

While Jay-Z was weighing the offer, worth between $8 million and $10 million per year depending on performance bonuses, Warner tried to lure him with a job overseeing all of the company's labels at a salary higher than the one offered by Def Jam, plus a substantial cut of Warner's upcoming initial public offering. But Def Jam had one thing Warner didn't—the rights to Jay-Z's master recordings. Under Def Jam's contract, his masters would revert to him within ten years. "It's an offer you can't refuse," Jay-Z said of the Def Jam deal. "I could say to my son or my daughter, or my nephews if I never have kids, 'Here's my whole collection of recordings. I own those, they're yours.'"[16]

Though a boon to his progeny, the deal was almost guaranteed to deal a fatal blow to Jay-Z's relationship with Roc-A-Fella cofounders Damon Dash and Kareem Burke. As president of Def Jam, which had purchased the trio's remaining stake in Roc-A-Fella for $10 million earlier in 2004, Jay-Z would become the de facto boss of his former partners. Their relationship was already strained, thanks in part to Dash's impetuousness and Jay-Z's growing desire to be seen as a legitimate businessman in his own right. In the waning days of 2004, Jay-Z invited Dash to dinner and informed him of his decision to accept Def Jam's offer. Not one to waste an opportunity to deliver a mafioso punchline, he told Dash that the decision was "just business."[17]

At best, Jay-Z's move was simply an example of someone accepting an enticing business offer. At worst, it was a corporate end-around on Dash. So, in what he called a gesture of goodwill, Jay-Z offered Dash and Burke full control of the Roc-A-Fella name in exchange for exclusive rights to the masters of *Reasonable Doubt*, which the trio co-owned. In Jay-Z's mind, Dash and Burke owned Boardwalk, and he was trying to give them Park Place for Marvin Gardens, but his offer was rejected. "I was like, let me try to figure out some way where everyone can be happy . . . let me get *Reasonable Doubt* and I'll give up [Roc-A-Fella]," Jay-Z said in 2005. "I thought it was more than fair . . . And when that was turned down, I had to make a choice. I'll leave that for the people to say what choice they would've made."[18]

Within weeks, Dash bolted Roc-A-Fella to start his own Universal imprint, Damon Dash Music Group. Under this agreement, he wouldn't have had to report to Jay-Z. But the deal fell apart amid reports that Dash had angered executives by constantly campaigning for a higher post within Universal.[19] In a separate deal, Jay-Z bought Dash's stake in Rocawear for $22 million,[20] severing the pair's remaining business ties. When the two encountered each other in an elevator shortly thereafter, the awkwardness was palpable. "If I were ever to write a movie, this would have to be either the end of it or the serious point when you know things have changed," Dash explained. "He had on a suit with shoes and a trench coat. And I had on my State Property [shirt] and my hat to the side. And it was like we were two different people. It was ill. Our conversation was brief, wasn't no malice, but we honestly were two different people. He was not the same person I had met. I would never expect him to wear a trench coat and shoes. It can just show that people can go in two totally separate directions."[21]

For Jay-Z, the split was partially a matter of efficiency. As the pair drifted apart in the years leading up to 2004, Jay-Z had identified a more effective right-hand man: his former accountant John Meneilly. "John is an incredibly smart guy. So is Damon," Jay-Z explained to *XXL* in 2009. "Dame is good at starting something. I don't know if he gets in his own way at a certain point. You know, the fights you had coming up aren't the same fights when you're on a different level. What would happen is, a lot of times, I would have to go fix. You know, it was time-consuming, going back and just doing three meetings, when we could have had one. Nothing got accomplished because everyone was screaming at each other."[22]

Though it may well have been warranted, Jay-Z's repudiation of Dash was yet another example of a common trend between Jay-Z and his erstwhile mentors and business partners. Just as he honed his lyrical skills with Jaz-O's help as a teenager in Brooklyn and developed his hustler's sense selling crack with DeHaven Irby in Trenton, he learned legitimate entrepreneurialism from Damon Dash. In each case,

Jay-Z absorbed the best qualities of his mentor, applied his own considerable talents to the subject at hand, quickly surpassed his mentor, and moved "on to the next one," fittingly the title of a song on his 2009 album, *The Blueprint 3*.

Unlike his very public separation from Dash, Jay-Z's disengagement from both Irby and Jaz-O received little attention from the mainstream media. Irby's disappearance from Jay-Z's life was hastened by the former's frequent jail stints; Irby claims that Jay-Z started trying to avoid him in the late 1990s.[23] Jaz-O stayed in Jay-Z's life longer than Irby, serving as a producer on *Reasonable Doubt* and remaining on good terms until 2002, when his relationship soured while recording a song with Jay-Z. "I asked him for like a verse and a half," says Jaz-O. "He was like, 'Nah, that's too much.'"[24] The elder rapper then took offense at comments made by Jay-Z's sidekick Memphis Bleek, assuming that Jay-Z had authorized them; Jay-Z and Jaz-O have been trading lyrical barbs ever since. One-liners from Jay-Z include "I'ma let karma catch up to Jaz-O"[25] and "nobody paid Jaz's wack ass,"[26] a snipe at his mentor's financial success as a rapper. Jaz-O released a slew of songs including the venomous "Ova," a play on both the word *over* and Jay-Z's Hova nickname. The track featured a few personal shots: "Your problems ain't ova, you're damaged, pa / I couldn't shoot my brother unless he was beatin' on ma / You's a fake friend, ova, my patience is ova."[27]

Jaz-O's complaints about Jay-Z are even more specific in conversation than they are in song. "When you start making money, you start loving the lifestyle, and in turn you start loving the money," he says. "Some people have the where-withal to put things in proper perspective, and some people become maniacal. I think in his case, to an extent, he became maniacal. He loves money. Truth be told, he's been willing to step on or step over anyone in his way whether they be friends, family, both, or neither, to acquire more."[28]

In the mind of DJ Clark Kent, however, the split between Jay-Z and his various mentors was simply the result of people growing in different directions. "When you meet some-body at age eighteen or nineteen, at twenty or twenty-five," he says, "twelve to fifteen years later, you're not the same people. So the people that they were just became too differ-ent to coexist. They were in different places. I think that's all that happened."[29]

═══

As Jay-Z was unwinding relationships with former associ-ates and preparing to transition from a career focused on music to a career focused on business, he found himself con-fronting someone he thought he'd never see again. In 2003, before the release of *The Black Album*, Jay-Z's mother discov-ered that his father, Adnis Reeves, was terminally ill. Despite the circumstances, Jay-Z was reluctant to come face-to-face with Reeves, but his mother arranged a meeting anyway. Reeves didn't show up. Undaunted, Jay-Z's mother organized a second meeting, and this time her son was finally able to confront the man who'd abandoned him as a boy nearly twenty-five years earlier.

"Me and my pop got to talk," Jay-Z told *Rolling Stone* in 2005. "That was very defining of my life. I got to let it go. I got to tell him everything I wanted to say. I just said what I felt. It wasn't yelling and crying and drastic and dramatic. It was very adult and grown men, but it was tough. I didn't let him off the hook. I was real tough with him. We just went through that whole thing. How could you do that? He was like, 'Well, you knew where I was. I was like, 'I'm a kid. I'm not supposed to find you. What are you talking about?' He said, 'You're right.' And then it was cool and that kinda freed everything."[30]

Jay-Z never revealed what precisely was freed by his paternal reconciliation, but clearly the interaction was monumental. When Jay-Z's father passed away a few months later, the rapper had already pardoned him in his own mind. "So, pop, I forgive you for all the shit that I lived through," he raps on "Moment of Clarity," a track on *The Black Album*. "It wasn't all your fault, homie, you got caught into the same game I fought . . . I'm just glad we got to see each other, talk, and remeet each other / Save a place in heaven 'til the next time we meet, forever."[31]

In the wake of his father's death and the closure brought by reconciliation, Jay-Z seemed to let down his guard, at least to a few of the people closest to him. Though the outward aloofness and aura of invincibility that he'd cultivated throughout his early career were still there, it's worth noting that Jay-Z's relationship with Beyoncé didn't begin to flourish until after he made amends with his father in 2003. Similarly, in the wake of the reunion, he stopped jettisoning mentors. Those who guided him through the middle of his career—Cohen, Meneilly, and marketing guru Steve Stoute, for example—were spared the fate of Jaz-O and Damon Dash.

He has also remained loyal to his protégés—including Memphis Bleek, who isn't the world's most gifted rapper but is a close friend of Jay-Z, and Kanye West, an unquestionably brilliant artist whose antics have nevertheless managed to alienate many supporters (Jay-Z even stood behind him during the Taylor Swift fiasco while millions were calling for Kanye's head). Perhaps reuniting with his father inspired Jay-Z to take on a paternal role in these relationships.

Whatever peace of mind the reunion brought Jay-Z, it couldn't possibly have prepared him for the next step in his career—running Def Jam—a task that proved to be much tougher than he'd anticipated.

6

Def Jam Takeover

If Jay-Z had 99 Problems in 2003, the quantity of his concerns must have swelled to triple digits when he took the helm at Def Jam on January 3, 2005. Prior to his arrival, the label had lost a litany of talent—Brooklyn-based rap group the Beastie Boys and Def Jam cofounder Rick Rubin left in the late 1980s, while seminal hip-hop squad Public Enemy and cofounder Russell Simmons departed in the late 1990s. (Simmons sold his remaining 40 percent stake in Def Jam for $100 million in 1999, a number no doubt boosted by the success of the Brooklyn-born rapper on the cover of this book.)[1]

Jay-Z inherited the difficult task of revitalizing the legendary label in an era of sagging record sales and shrinking budgets. Like much of the industry, Def Jam's payroll was stacked with relics of the 1980s. "The culture there has been institu-tionalized," Jay-Z told *Rolling Stone* in 2010. "You had record executives there who've been sitting in their office for twenty years because of one act. 'But that's the guy who signed Möt-ley Crüe!' Seriously? That was twenty-five years ago."[2]

Demoralized by what he found at Def Jam, Jay-Z came close to breaking his "I will not lose, ever" vow early in his tenure as president. "I wanted to quit right away," he said in 2005. "There was nothing fresh, there was no excitement, it was just doing the same shit over again. I said, 'Where's the passion? Where's the ideas? Where's the new shit?' I'm used to being around entrepreneurs and we was passionate about everything. But whether this artist comes out and [sells] four hundred million or forty thousand [albums] the first week, [the average employee's] check is the same. So you're doing everything routine, routine, routine, and you lose the pas-sion for it. You stop coming up with new ideas, and you start erasing the name off the marketing plan and fill it in with another name and it's the same shit."[3]

Jay-Z revved up his employees by calling for a two-day retreat at Manhattan's Tribeca Grand Hotel. He gave a speech, then played a tape of Def Jam's 1984 sales pitch to give his workers a reminder of the label's fiery, independent roots. Then he went around the room and asked staffers to share their reasons for getting into the record business in the first place. "We got people to go back to that inner kid and the joy of being in the record business," he said. "I wanted them to be alive again."[4]

DEF JAM TAKEOVER 99

His focus on making his employees feel good about their jobs wasn't limited to theatrics at posh hotels. Though Jay-Z's lyrical boasts could make Donald Trump cringe—there's a line where Jay-Z calls himself "God MC"—he proved to be a humble and introspective boss. In a spoken word interlude to one of Jay-Z's songs, his Brooklyn buddy Biggie says, "The key to staying on top of things is to treat everything like it's your first project, know what I'm saying? Like it's your first day like when you was an intern . . . stay humble."[5] Many who worked with Jay-Z at Def Jam say he embodied that philosophy, from the label's top artists all the way down to interns like Nick Simmons, an aspiring entertainment executive who worked at Def Jam in the summer between his sophomore and junior years of college. "Jay would walk by and say, 'Hey, how ya doing,'" Simmons remembers. "Sometimes he'd come over to the intern booth just to say hi."[6]

Those who crossed paths with Jay-Z in the boardroom noticed a keen intellectual curiosity in the Def Jam president. "One of the things I like about the guy is that he wants to learn," says Bernie Resnick, a Philadelphia-based entertainment lawyer. "He has a thirst for knowledge. And even when he was younger, he was always asking questions. If it was backstage or in a studio or a business meeting, he wasn't afraid to say, 'Hey, how does this work?' Or, 'What's the structure of that kind of deal?' He was always very curious about business deals. Which lends itself well to someone who would like to transition from being an artist to being a business impresario."[7]

Jay-Z's new boss, Antonio "L.A." Reid, wasn't shy about heaping praise on his star employee. "Being around Jay is inspirational to people," he gushed to *Billboard* in 2006. "I don't care if you're a forty-year-old executive or a twenty-year-old intern—having that kind of access to that kind of wisdom, stardom, experience, and level of charm could change your life."[8]

Though he proved to be more than capable as a schmoozer, Jay-Z's main task as president was to beef up Def Jam's sagging musical lineup. One of his first signings was Barbadian singer Rihanna. A multiplatinum Grammy winner today, she was a nervous seventeen-year-old when she auditioned at Def Jam's New York offices in 2005. As soon as she sang "Pon de Replay," which eventually became her first big hit, Jay-Z recognized her potential and signed her to a record deal the same night. "The audition definitely went well," Rihanna recalled in 2007. "Jay-Z said, 'There's only two ways out. Out the door after you sign this deal, or through this window.' And we were on the twenty-ninth floor. Very flattering."[9]

While Rihanna went about recording her debut album, Jay-Z encountered some setbacks—both personal and professional. Over the years, he'd grown close to his nephew, Colleek Luckie; when he nearly missed Luckie's high school graduation in 2005 because of a cab snafu, Jay-Z made a rare show of emotion ("I was so mad," he said. "I had tears in my eyes and shit. I don't cry over nothing."[10]) Though he made it to the ceremony, devastating news came weeks later: Luckie was killed in a car accident while sitting in the passenger

DEF JAM TAKEOVER   **101**

seat of the Chrysler that Jay-Z had given him as a graduation present. When asked about the incident in 2005, Jay-Z was noticeably shaken. "It was the toughest shit," he said. "Nothing close to it. Like I'm numb. I'm numb."[11] His nephew's passing represented not only the loss of a bright young life, but perhaps also the interruption of Jay-Z's attempts to deal with his own feelings of paternal abandonment by acting as a father figure to Luckie.

Back at the office, Jay-Z kept his composure in spite of the additional adversity. Albums from Marcy chum Memphis Bleek and Philadelphia-based rap duo Young Gunz produced dreary sales numbers despite heavy shilling from Jay-Z himself. So he set about signing more acts to Def Jam. The Roots, one of hip-hop's edgiest acts, were among the new additions. Their relationship with Jay-Z dated back to 2001, when the group agreed to work as Jay-Z's backup band on the live album *MTV Unplugged: Jay-Z*.

On a winter's day too snowy for an in-person interview, the group's drummer, Questlove, recalls that he was a bit skeptical when the Roots first hooked up with Jay-Z. Unlike the alternative Roots, Jay-Z—especially in the old days—was known for being an ultra-materialist with a penchant for rapping about guns and money. But Questlove soon discovered the man behind the image. "Jay constantly wanted to figure out how to better his situation," he explains. "He would stay in rehearsal until very late. And he would ask a lot of questions. And he would show up on time . . . He's the easiest artist I've ever worked with. He's literally trying to better his art, which was surprisingly admirable to me. Because I just figured, 'Oh, you're the king of the hill, why would you even give a fuck about your art? Who cares about art when you've got money?' "[12]

Impressed with Jay-Z's inquisitive nature, the group turned to him when they started looking for a new home in 2005, picking Def Jam over other labels and more lucrative terms. They felt lost in the shuffle at Jimmy Iovine's Interscope Records and believed Jay-Z would be a much more attentive boss. Thanks to the tremendous respect Iovine had for Jay-Z, the Def Jam president was able to facilitate the Roots' release from Interscope without wounding any egos. "I told Jay, 'I wanna come to Def Jam,' and he was like, 'All right, cool,'" explains the ever-mellow Questlove. "So he asked Jimmy Iovine. And we wrote an e-mail . . . Like, 'We just want to transfer to Def Jam, is that okay?' And [Jimmy] said, 'Hey, that was the most respectful release I've ever done.' "[13]

Less than a year later, the Roots found themselves in a bind that required the sort of personal attention that drew them to Def Jam in the first place. This situation was so dicey and urgent that it seemed not even Jay-Z could fix it: on the eve of finalizing their latest album, the Roots discovered they needed legal approval to use a sample from a song by the rock band Radiohead. "We had exactly twenty-four hours to get an impossible clearance," recalls Questlove. "We were pulling our hair out because this was like the emotional centerpiece of the album, and now we're about to lose this because the lawyers are like, 'No, we want $700,000.' Which was unheard of." So Questlove called Jay-Z and explained the situation. "'Please tell me you know anybody in Radiohead,'" he remembers telling Jay-Z. "He's like, 'I'll see what I can do.' I was like, 'Fuck, we're going to lose this song.' Amazingly, while I'm at the gym an hour later, [Radiohead lead singer] Thom Yorke gives us a call, and you know, it was quite the opposite. They were really flattered that we considered it, and he approved it."

With the sample approved, the Roots' *Game Theory* went on to sell sixty-one thousand copies in its first week,[14] a respectable figure for a band that had always been more of an artistic act than a pop sensation. Jay-Z encouraged the group to stay true to that philosophy. "The pressure that you would think would be on us, i.e., 'I want that radio song, don't come in here unless you've got a hit,' was the exact opposite," remembers Questlove. "Jay was like, 'You'd better give me the art record I expect from you guys, because I'm gonna have the whole world out to castrate me if I change their beloved Roots.'" Sure enough, the Roots' album made up in critical reception what it lacked in sales. The album earned four stars out of four from *USA Today*, which applauded the Roots for exhibiting "a ferocity they haven't displayed in years";[15] positive reviews also flowed in from *Rolling Stone* and the *Village Voice*, the latter of which specifically praised Jay-Z for not making the Roots "go commercial."[16]

Jay-Z had other artists to lean on for raw sales, and by the end of his first summer as Def Jam's chief, those numbers started to show. Kanye West and Young Jeezy both put out albums that went platinum with Jay-Z's help; Rihanna's debut sold five hundred thousand copies in six months, as did the rookie effort of rapper Rick Ross, another Jay-Z recruit, in 2006.[17] Perhaps just as important as the songs released by these artists were the songs held back. When Kanye West was putting together his first album, Jay-Z implored him not to include a song called "Hey Mama," fearing it would get lost in the shuffle of West's debut. On his mentor's advice, West saved the track, and it helped propel his next offering, *Late Registration*, to triple-platinum sales and a Grammy award for Best Rap Album.

Nurturing the careers of these artists was one of Jay-Z's great successes during his time at Def Jam, and his peers in the executive ranks took note. "It was definitely something that you saw, his skills as an executive and his skills as a creative A&R [artists and repertoire] person," says Craig Kallman, chief executive of Atlantic Records. "He certainly masterminded the Rihanna signing and launch and creatively spearheaded that. He oversaw Rick Ross and galvanized the company behind Rick. I think he did a great job."[18]

In early 2006, Jay-Z made perhaps his boldest move by reconciling with former nemesis Nas and signing the rapper to Def Jam, banking that defusing their conflict would sell more records than fanning the flames. As noted earlier, the two performed in concert together in 2005, much to the surprise of a crowd expecting Jay-Z to ratchet up the rivalry's rhetoric. Nas's initial Def Jam effort, *Hip-Hop Is Dead*, hit stores a year later. Jay-Z appeared on the track "Black Republicans," and the album sold an impressive 355,000 copies in its first week.[19]

"If you ask me to grade my performance as the president, I'd say A-plus," Jay-Z boasted in a 2009 interview. "No one can bat 1.000. It's impossible. I mean, everyone is looking at my shit. But if we really looked under the hood [of every record executive] and the acts they put out at the time, I'd be comparable to anyone."[20]

Though Jay-Z sometimes gives his audience the impression that business is more important to him than rap ("I'm just a hustler disguised as a rapper," he claims in one song[21]), many people who've spent time with him believe his heart is in music. Patrick "A Kid Called Roots" Lawrence, who produced the hit song "Do My . . ." for Memphis Bleek, recalls witnessing Jay-Z's passion firsthand in 2000.

Lawrence had been dispatched to Japan by Lyor Cohen, then-chief of Def Jam, to help start the label's Japanese division. In the midst of Lawrence's three-month stay in Tokyo, Jay-Z came to the city for the first time to perform a concert. When the rapper noticed Lawrence at the show, he invited him to come onstage. Lawrence obliged and couldn't help but notice that the five thousand Japanese fans in the audience— many of whom didn't speak English at all—knew all the words to Jay-Z's songs. After his first set, Jay-Z took a break and let Memphis Bleek perform a few songs, including Lawrence's "Do My . . ." Lawrence would never have expected what came next.

"Jay-Z pulls me to the edge of the stage . . . and for three minutes I perform 'Do My . . .' with Jay-Z and Memphis Bleek," Lawrence recalls. "Incredible. It was like a dream. I mean, the energy. Now I see why, with all his success and his money—he claims he's just a hustler—at the end of the day, he really has a passion for the music. He loves it, he thrives for that feeling of being on that stage and seeing what that's like. 'Cause I really felt it right then. When I got off that stage, I was like, 'I want to be a rap star.' "[22]

Wanting to be a rap star again, and feeling that rush anew, was ultimately what drew Jay-Z back to the microphone in 2006. A desire to prop up sales at Def Jam, not to mention the constant desire to add funds to his own ballooning bank account, obviously contributed to Jay-Z's decision as well. And for someone who'd stopped releasing solo albums three years earlier because he was bored with hip-hop, the opportunity to ride in on a white horse as the industry's savior was too tempting to pass up.

His comeback album, *Kingdom Come*, hit stores in November 2006 and sold over two million copies in its first three weeks. "I don't know what life will be in H-I-P-H-O-P without the boy H-O-V," he crows at the start of the album's title track, referencing his lordly nickname. "Not only N-Y-C, but hip-hop's savior / So after this flow, you might owe me a favor, when Kingdom Come."[23] Despite decent commercial success and his own blustering bravado, Jay-Z's new album earned him some of the roughest reviews of his career, not to mention a few barbs about his age. "We never thought Jay would be flashing AARP brochures in our faces and dropping Gwyneth Paltrow's name in a rap song," raged Pitchfork's Peter Macia in a review. "But that's *Kingdom Come:* Jay boringly rapping about boring stuff and being totally comfortable with it."[24]

Perhaps because he was itching to redeem himself, perhaps because he just wanted to make another album, Jay-Z quickly followed *Kingdom Come* with another, grittier album in 2007. That summer, Jay-Z attended a private screening of Ridley Scott's *American Gangster* (coincidentally, the event was set up by his aforementioned intern, Simmons). Inspired by the film's content—the rise and fall of 1970s Harlem drug kingpin Frank Lucas, played by Denzel Washington—Jay-Z churned out an album of the same title in a matter of weeks. Falling back from the name-dropping and soft subject matter of *Kingdom Come*, Jay-Z returned to the mafioso mentality that birthed his first album. That was clear from the opening line of *American Gangster*'s first song: "Mind state of a gangster from the forties meets the business mind of Motown's Berry Gordy / Turn crack rock into a chain of 40/40s," he raps, not forgetting to toss in some free advertising for his nightclubs. "America, meet the gangster Shawn Corey. Hey, young world, wanna hear a story? Close your eyes, and you could pretend you're me."[25]

The rest of the album told that story. This time, the critical response was much warmer. "He packs his wordy stanzas full of unexpected syllables, clever allusions, and unpredictable rhyme schemes," declared the *New York Times.* "This is probably as close as the new Jay-Z will ever come to sounding like the old Jay-Z."[26] A few days later *Rolling Stone* proclaimed, "Forget Frank Lucas: the real black superhero here is Jay, and with *American Gangster,* [he's] back."[27] On the album, Jay-Z painted himself as an analog to Denzel Washington's Frank Lucas in *American Gangster*: clever, pragmatic, unflappable. Those who spent significant time with Jay-Z during this phase of his career tend to reinforce the comparison. "I've never really seen this guy sweat," explained Gimel "Young Guru" Keaton, a former Roc-A-Fella sound engineer, in 2009. "That's a running joke that we have: he's an alien, because I've never seen him sweat . . . I've never seen Jay super angry, or he doesn't show it. It's always the poker face."[28]

The major exception to that rule was the Lance Rivera stabbing of 1999. Jay-Z was lucky to strike a plea deal that didn't include jail time; in *Vibe*'s December 2000 cover story, he called the incident a "learning experience." Apparently it was. Weeks before *American Gangster* hit the stores in 2007, tracks from the album leaked. Though he was upset, Jay-Z found himself playing the role of coolheaded boss at Def Jam. "People were panicking," recalls Simmons. "But I never heard [Jay-Z] yell or flip out or anything. He's just an even-keel kind of guy." Or at least, he'd learned how to be an even-keel kind of guy in the years following the Rivera incident.

Though Jay-Z attended a single therapy session (he said all

the psychiatrist did was give him tea that made him sleepy),[29] there were a number of external factors that took some pressure off him in the years between the two leaks. There was reconciliation with his father, stability with Beyoncé, and security in his status at the top of the hip-hop world. Coupled with the effects of time and experience, the Jay-Z of 2007 was quite a different person from the Jay-Z of 1999. "I think he just grew up," says Simmons. "He even says it in his songs: I used to be the dude wearing jerseys and stuff, but now I'm a businessman. I gotta get corporate. I gotta put on a suit and a button-up shirt."

Jay-Z had mastered his own emotions, transforming the vengeful urges of his youth into the sort of unflappability that would prove invaluable in the boardroom. With that change—and the wealth of executive experience he'd gained at Def Jam—he found a world of new business opportunities available to him. Jay-Z's polish and poise would eventually take him to corporate pastures even greener than Def Jam, but in the meantime, he turned his attention to something quite literally related to green pastures and fields: the champagne industry.

Champagne Secrets

On a frigid February night, I'm waiting outside the door of a ground-floor apartment in Harlem, beginning to wonder if I've got the wrong address. The barred windows on either side of me are dark. In the middle of the door, a large Black Panther logo obscures a glass pane that rattles faintly as the subway grumbles below. I ring the bell for a third time. No response.

Suddenly, a voice calls my name. I turn around. Striding toward me amid a majestic cascade of dreadlocks is Branson B., the man credited with introducing champagne to hip-hop. He gave rap legend Notorious B.I.G. his first taste of Cristal, the $500-a-bottle French bubbly that quickly joined Mercedes-Benz and Gucci as rap's most frequently mentioned brands. Branson himself has been mentioned in over sixty songs.

(Appropriately for rap's unofficial sommelier, the abbreviated *B* is short for Belchie.[1])

Branson greets me with a handshake and a chest bump and opens the door. We enter a dim foyer stacked to the ceiling with case upon case of his personal label of Guy Charlemagne wine. He leads the way through another door into a room dominated by a full-sized bar. "I made it myself," he says, pulling up a pair of stools. Then he disappears back into the foyer.

I feel like I've fallen through a rabbit hole into an oenophilic wonderland. Scattered before me are at least twenty bottles of wine and champagne in varying states of consumption; dozens more adorn the shelves behind the counter. Resting on a table next to the bar is a plasterboard sign with the words BRANSON B. CUVÉE emblazoned over the silhouette of a dreadlocked man. The walls are coated with cutouts from wine publications. A deflated purple birthday balloon hangs in the corner.

Branson bustles back into the room, the foil neck of a champagne bottle peeking out over the rim of the ice bucket in his arms. "One of Jay-Z's favorite drinks is the Taittinger Rosé Comtes—we called that the 'Food of the Gods,'" he says, recalling the rare $300 bottle made from France's finest Chardonnay grapes. "One time I remember I came in, and Biggie and Jay were in the studio, and they had a bottle on the table, and Jay kind of looked at me and smiled because he knew it was something I introduced him to."

Branson puts down the bucket and lowers himself onto the stool next to me.

"Last time I seen Jay, he said, 'Damn, every time I see you, I think about Biggie,'" Branson continues. "I always used to come through and bring them different things, and we used to sit around and drink together and enjoy," he says. "They'd be like, 'Yo, this is good.' And it seemed to be a thing of, 'Damn, I've never seen this before, never tasted this before!' 'Cause it's new."

Still glancing around the room, my eyes fall on an empty gold bottle of Armand de Brignac, another trendy $300 champagne. "Respectfully, I didn't care for it," Branson pipes in, as if reading my mind. "I didn't think it was worth the money. When I initially tasted it, it was a little young, so I really didn't like it."

He gestures to a neighboring bottle whose ridged surface makes it look like the love child of an armadillo and a grenade. "This is a Nicolas Feuillatte Palmes d'Or Rosé, 1999," he says. "I happened to go to a liquor store in New Jersey, and I was looking for something special for my birthday, and I ran into that. I really enjoyed it. It was nice, and it was different."

"This," he says, pointing back to the gilded Armand de Brignac, "is more the aesthetics, the pretty bottle—and everything that goes along with it."

What goes along with Armand de Brignac is Jay-Z. The rapper put the flashy gold bottle on the map when he featured it in his 2006 video for "Show Me What You Got," a single from his comeback album *Kingdom Come.* The four-minute video begins with a shot of a car parked on a bluff overlooking Monaco. The camera pans in to reveal Jay-Z sitting in a Ferrari F430 Spyder convertible, his foot hanging nonchalantly over the side. An exotic Pagani Zonda roadster pulls up next to him, piloted by IndyCar driver Danica Patrick.

"What you got?" Jay-Z asks Patrick, adjusting his sunglasses. Then he leans back to reveal his driver: NASCAR veteran Dale Earnhardt Jr.

The music begins, Patrick shrugs, and the two cars zoom off in a mountainside race inspired by the opening sequence of the James Bond flick *GoldenEye.* Later in the video, Jay-Z arrives at a rollicking party on what appears to be a private island. As the third verse begins, he raps about the "gold bottles of the Ace of Spades." He then becomes embroiled in a high-stakes game of blackjack with swimsuit model Jarah Mariano, who's holding two queens. Jay-Z, naturally, has both the king and ace of spades. The video fades into an orgy of belly dancing, hand waving, and other forms of enjoyment presumably available only to those who attend parties at medium-size private islands off the coast of Monaco (though a quick search on Google Earth reveals that there are, in fact, no such islands off the coast of Monaco).

The video is typical of mainstream hip-hop, with one possible exception: toward the end of the video, a waiter presents Jay-Z with a bottle of Cristal champagne, and Jay-Z declines with a sweep of his hand. In its place, he accepts a gold bottle of then-unknown Armand de Brignac. This may not seem

terribly meaningful in the abstract, but coming from someone who'd been rapping Cristal's praises for years—and
once bragged that he was "popping that Cristal when all y'all
thought it was beer"[2]—it marked a major departure.

Jay-Z's sudden change in attitude toward the pricey bubbly wasn't without cause. In June 2006, months before the
video's release, a reporter from the *Economist* asked Frédéric Rouzaud, manager of the Louis Roederer house that
produces Cristal, what he thought of rappers drinking his
champagne. "That's a good question," Rouzaud replied. "But
what can we do? We can't forbid people from buying it. I'm
sure Dom Pérignon or Krug would be delighted to have their
business."[3]

As soon as Jay-Z caught wind of the comments, he publicly
denounced Rouzaud. Cristal was one of the only brands Jay-Z
had been willing to promote for free in his songs, but a slight
of this nature was grounds for a boycott. "It has come to my
attention that the managing director of Cristal, Frédéric Rouzaud, views the hip-hop culture as 'unwelcome attention,'" he
declared. "I view his comments as racist and will no longer
support any of his products through any of my various brands
including the 40/40 Club nor in my personal life."[4]

The mainstream media joined industry observers to weigh
in on Jay-Z's statement. "Don't drop a bomb like 'racist'
when what you're dealing with is a skirmish over image," the
Washington Post admonished.[5] "Hell hath no fury like a rap
impresario dissed," noted Slate.[6] Roberto Rogness, an NPR
commentator and general manager of Santa Monica's Wine

Expo, offered another suggestion: "If Jay-Z *really* wanted to show them what for, he should buy Roederer and give it to Beyoncé for a wedding present!"[7]

Meanwhile, Cristal's golden image was starting to tarnish. Though demand continued to outpace supply worldwide, Jay-Z's boycott had a noticeable effect on sales. "I've noticed a slight drop-off in Cristal in the club," said Noel Ashman, owner of Manhattan's Plumm, a favorite celebrity nightspot. "You have to recognize how deeply respected Jay-Z is, so his position definitely will have an effect."[8] Though Jay-Z initially replaced Cristal with Krug and Dom Pérignon in his clubs as Rouzaud had mockingly suggested, the release of the "Show Me What You Got" video on October 10 immediately established Armand de Brignac as his favorite. The use of the "Ace of Spades" moniker—a possible reclamation of the word *spade*, a slur used against African Americans—can also be seen as a clever swipe at Rouzaud's perceived racism.

By simply associating himself with Armand de Brignac, Jay-Z was able to almost single-handedly lift the brand from obscurity to the heights of celebrity chic. Proprietors of many American liquor stores reported that sales of Armand de Brignac were quickly catching up to the older bubbly. "Our sales of Armand de Brignac are rivaling Cristal," said Christian Navarro, a shop owner in Brentwood, California. "They've managed to shortcut one hundred and fifty years of traditional marketing."[9]

Some observers pointed out that Armand de Brignac, which shared its first four letters with Jay-Z's Armadale

se of its very sweet taste, something frowned upon by
connoisseurs. The champagne's sweetness comes from
what's known as a high dosage. Toward the end of the
agne-making process, a mixture of white wine, brandy,
gar—the dosage—is added to fermented champagne.
xact amount added is up to the producer; low dosage
the dry champagne favored by wine experts, while
losage produces sweeter champagne. "That's why
nd de Brignac] is popular among the hip-hop com-
, because it has a high dosage," says Fass. "Cristal is a
rful wine. But wine people, if they say there's one thing
t, it might be that it's a little bit too sweet."

was working at a store in midtown Manhattan called
Wine & Spirits when Armand de Brignac came out
. Though the large store frequently ordered cases of
Moët & Chandon, and other fine champagnes, Armand
gnac was never on their list. "We would not touch
nd de Brignac] because we knew this was a scam,"
ss. "It could have been easy money. We couldn't do it.
ldn't pull the trigger. It was just such a transparently
bullshit thing that was going on."

sponse to such criticism, employees of Cattier, the
house that produces Armand de Brignac, like to tout
ampagne's accolades.[15] In December 2009, for exam-
was named the world's best-tasting champagne by
ampagne magazine. To win the Fine award, Armand
nac bested one thousand other champagnes. Fass
mpressed. "I saw that online, and I think it's pitooey,

Vodka, could be Jay-Z's latest business venture. He wasn't
shy about his connection to the spirit, but that product
flopped; the last major news story about the vodka came in
2005, when a case disappeared en route to Mariah Carey's
birthday party.[10] In the wake of Jay-Z's split with Dash and
Burke, there was no chance he'd enrich his former partners
by rapping about Armadale (the spirit has since vanished
from the public eye and store shelves altogether, and the U.S.
Patent and Trademark Office database has listed the brand
as "DEAD" since May 2, 2009[11]).

By 2006, Jay-Z was clearly on the lookout for a new bever-
age to hawk. Pundits theorized that he could have dreamed
up Armand de Brignac to capitalize on his own Cristal boycott, and the stealth with which he promoted the champagne
was simply a change in marketing strategy after overhyping
Armadale. "Anytime you're promoting a product, you're trying to convince the public that it's part of your lifestyle," says
Ryan Schinman, founder of Platinum Rye, the world's largest
buyer of media for corporations. "The minute that the public
thinks that it's part of your lifestyle because it's a paid situation, it doesn't help the cause." Schinman points to McDon-
ald's ill-fated plan, launched in 2005, to pay rappers up to $5
for every radio spin of any song in which they mentioned the
Big Mac. "The minute it came out," he says, "it was inauthen-
tic and the whole program was worthless."[12]

Accordingly, two days after the gold bottle's inclusion in
Jay-Z's "Show Me What You Got" video, Armand de Brignac attempted to dispel rumors of a financial connection to

Jay-Z. Representatives issued a press release explaining that the champagne was simply an "ultra-luxury product in the high-end champagne category" that was "making its North American debut this year, after enjoying success as a premium, high-end brand in France."[13]

═

Amid the aftermath of the divorce between Jay-Z and Cristal, Branson B.—the self-described street entrepreneur who'd introduced the star-crossed lovers nearly two decades earlier through the Notorious B.I.G.—found himself in France, hand-selecting grapes for his own Branson B. Cuvée champagne. During the three months he spent in the heart of wine country, he never heard a peep about Armand de Brignac or Ace of Spades. The notion that it had enjoyed "success as a premium, high-end brand in France" just wasn't true.

"Didn't exist," Branson explains, fishing a bottle of Nicolas Feuillatte Brut from an ice bucket. He pops the bottle and fills two champagne flutes.

"Life," he says.

"L'chaim," I return, clinking his glass.

"How do you like this?" he asks after my first sip.

"It's nice," I reply. "I'm kind of an amateur, but it tastes less dry than others I've had."

"Lightly fruity?"

"Almost like a white wine."

"Like a chardonnay?"

"Yeah," I reply, suddenly self-cons
accurate?"

"I recognized what you said." He
accurate."

Branson glances back at the bottl

"You look at these pretty bottles,
pour something out, it's going to ta
special," he says. "Now if you're use
and you pour something out of tha
no place, you're going to be disapp
and you didn't enjoy it, and you wa
know what I mean?"

I nod, recalling the first time I ta
light, sweet, and altogether decent,

"The ride didn't flip the way it s
the curve too slow, didn't turn up
seeming to read my mind. "When
of money, you want to be excited."

═

Jay-Z may tout Armand de Brign
but to some champagne industry
ocre product masquerading as a
biggest rip-off in the history of
independent wine buyer based in
shit. At least Cristal tastes good."
Fass explains that Armand de B

becau
most
havin
cham
and s
The
yields
high
[Arm
munit
wonde
about
Fas
Crush
in 200
Krug,
de Bri
[Arma
says F
We co
obviou
In
Frencl
their c
ple, it
Fine C
de Bri
wasn't

horseshit," he says. "Anybody who sits down and tastes a thousand champagnes, that's humanly impossible—your gums will be rotting and the enamel will be falling off your teeth. These wine tastings are garbage. But that's how a lot of secondary and crappy wines [market themselves], they win bronze medals or gold medals. Everybody has a wine tasting . . . There's a lot of stupid people in the world."[16]

On the quantitative side of the champagne world, Armand de Brignac tends to score in the low nineties on the industry-standard scale that goes up to one hundred. *Wine Spectator* gave it an eighty-eight in 2008.[17] That's still respectable, but well short of other high-priced champagnes like Cristal, whose various vintages often flirt with one hundred. Dom Pérignon, which can be had for $150, usually scores in the mid-nineties. Armand de Brignac's ratings place it on par with varieties of Veuve Clicquot and Taittinger that sell for $50 or less. Yet Armand de Brignac has sold 100 percent of every annual release of the $300 bottle; its highest annual unit volume thus far was forty-two thousand bottles. Representatives insist that demand for Armand de Brignac far outpaces the brand's maximum output of sixty thousand bottles per year.[18]

"Everybody should take a lesson who wants to sell wine that sucks," says Fass. "Because it is probably the most brilliant marketing in the history of wine . . . What an amazing job to take a piece of shit wine and turn it into a $300 bottle of wine overnight."[19]

So why would Jay-Z get involved with a second-tier champagne? Because of the immense profit potential. Unlike vodka, which also has low production costs but produces a narrower spectrum of tastes, the ceiling on prices for champagne is nearly unlimited. Fass estimates that Cattier's production cost for each $300 bottle of Armand de Brignac is a mere 10 euros (about $13). "The profit margin for that champagne is something I've never heard of before," says Fass. "Why would a profit margin be that high? Because there are a lot of [investors] to pay out."

Assuming Jay-Z is one of these people, the connection could be through any number of outlets: the house of Cattier itself, the brand Armand de Brignac, the importer, the exporter, or the distributor. All of these entities are registered with an array of state and national government agencies in the United States and France. Theoretically, the link could be established with a little bit of sleuth work.

My first call goes to the French offices of the Comité Interprofessionnel du Vin de Champagne, the trade association that includes all the grape growers and houses of Champagne, France. A woman named Brigitte informs me that Cattier is 100 percent family owned, but that the brand Armand de Brignac might have a different structure. She suggests trying the French department of agriculture. An e-mail to the agency yields a reply from one Isabelle Ruault, who explains that the brand Armand de Brignac is registered to AJC International, an export company owned by J. J. Cattier. Ruault supposes the brand belongs entirely to the family, but without knowing AJC's precise capital structure, the exact details are *impossible de savoir.*[20]

Turning my attention to stateside bureaucracies, I place a call to the Bureau of Alcohol, Tobacco, Firearms and Explosives in Washington, D.C. A representative redirects me to the Alcohol and Tobacco Tax and Trade Bureau, which in turn points me to the New York State Liquor Authority in Harlem. There, a man named Kashif Thompson informs me that Armand de Brignac is distributed by Sovereign Brands, LLC, and imported by Southern Wines & Spirits.[21] Southern is one of the largest liquor distributors in the country, and it's known for having personal relationships with some of the biggest names in hip-hop. Fass noted this firsthand while working at Crush: "50 Cent wanted magnums of Patrón tequila, which are incredibly rare, and the leader of Southern dropped them off to our store, and 50 Cent picked them up."[22] A call to the Florida Department of Business and Professional Regulation turns up a list of Southern's owners; Shawn Carter is not listed among them.

The last link is Sovereign Brands, whose owner is listed as Brett Berish. Berish, I later learn, is an entrepreneur who distributes and owns a line of spirits called 3 Vodka. The brand was launched in 2004 as a partnership with Atlanta-based hip-hop mogul Jermaine Dupri,[23] who overlapped with Jay-Z as a member of Island Def Jam's executive ranks. I also discover that shortly after Armand de Brignac's 2006 launch, Berish issued a press release saying that "Armand de Brignac and Jay-Z have not entered into any agreement, sponsorship or otherwise." However, he didn't specify whether there was a financial agreement between Sovereign and Jay-Z. Besides Berish, the only other owner listed for Armand de Brignac is Shannon Bullinger, Sovereign's operations manager. If Jay-Z has a Dupri-style partnership with Berish, it's not on the books.[24]

≡

Back at Branson's spot in Harlem, I've lost track of time. It's well past midnight, and our champagne flutes are nearly empty. We're still talking about Armand de Brignac.

"The funny thing," he says, considering the bottle, "is I *drank* that before."

He points across the bar to a bottle of Antique Gold, strikingly similar to the empty Armand de Brignac sitting in front of us. "That bottle there, a friend of mine brought it back from Monaco," he says. "It's like sixty dollars, seventy dollars, eighty dollars in the store."

He motions back to the Armand de Brignac.

"Armand de Brignac, this product already existed," he says. "They just brought this name back, and they attached Jay-Z to it."

I nod, realizing the magnitude of what Branson has just said. Antique Gold, the champagne Branson's friend brought back from Monaco, has been around for decades. Armand de Brignac, the one that started appearing in Jay-Z's videos circa 2006, looks nearly identical and costs five times as much. Both are made by Cattier—the only real difference seems to be the pewter Ace of Spades label slapped on the more expensive bottle.

Branson shuffles back behind the bar and starts to rummage around for something.

"So that means that they didn't have to go through a whole process [of starting a new brand]," he says. "Which would have taken about two years."

I empty my champagne flute.

Suddenly, Branson emerges with a sheaf of paper. My heart leaps. Could this be the document that establishes a paper trail between Jay-Z and Armand de Brignac?

"Jay and I have a relationship, we know one another," says Branson, sitting down. "And here it is, I have this champagne, I'd like for my champagne to be in his environments [where] he sells products. If he can bring Veuve Clicquot [to the 40/40 Club], why can't he bring Branson B. into his environment? That, I don't understand. I have no idea."

Branson shuffles through the stack and produces a coffee-stained sheet of paper. I crane my neck, hoping to catch a glimpse of a contract, a document with percentages. But it's something totally different. Addressed to Shawn "Jay-Z" Carter at the 40/40 Club, 6 West 25th Street, New York, New York, 10010, it's a copy of the letter that accompanied bottles of Branson B. Cuvée to Jay-Z's offices in 2006, shortly after Jay-Z announced his Cristal boycott.

"I checked to make sure they received the product," says Branson, continuing to leaf through the papers. "I didn't get a response from him."

Branson's words hang in the air for a poignant moment.

"I don't completely understand that," he says.

I nod sympathetically, but I completely understand. When it comes to business, Jay-Z is a cold pragmatist. He ditched Jaz-O, the boyhood mentor who showed him how to rhyme; he split with Damon Dash, the man who taught him how to sell CDs. He even shot his own brother in the shoulder for stealing his jewelry. Jay-Z parted ways with many of his former colleagues because he realized he'd outgrown them, or simply didn't need their help; there's no reason to expect he'd approach a champagne venture differently.

That said, working with Branson B. would have made sense in other ways. Jay-Z's champagne adventure started as a response to what he perceived as a racist statement by Roederer's Rouzaud about rap culture. What better way to prove him wrong than starting a champagne brand with hip-hop's own sommelier? Perhaps Branson's entreaties never made it past Jay-Z's gatekeepers. Certainly the duo could have come up with a more reasonably priced bubbly—Branson's retails for $40 to $75 per bottle. But there are very few people in the world who can inspire others to pay $300 for a bottle of champagne, and Jay-Z is apparently one of them. Partnering on a cheaper champagne would have meant a smaller profit to split, and thus, it would have been bad business for Jay-Z. In Branson's eyes, that's why it's so obvious that Jay-Z has a monetary stake in Armand de Brignac.

"I couldn't imagine that he wouldn't benefit financially," he says. "Why would he do that if he didn't have a financial stake? Why would he associate Shawn Carter with champagne and not benefit from it?"

My head swimming and my eyelids drooping, I stay for another ten minutes of small talk. Then I thank Branson for his hospitality and head out into the bitter February night.

Though my visit didn't yield a concrete paper trail between Jay-Z and Ace of Spades, and my calls to various government agencies in the United States and France had yielded only circumstantial evidence, there was one last chance: a transatlantic trip to the birthplace of Armand de Brignac.

The village of Chigny-Les-Roses, France, is so tiny that it seems nobody ever bothered to put street numbers on any of the buildings. Given the number of edifices in the town, it would be about as useful as numbering the pots and pans in one's kitchen. Fortunately, I'm already with the Cattier-employed guide who will take me to the company's champagne cellars.

We walk down Rue Dom Pérignon and stop in front of an unnumbered house with all its windows shuttered. The gate in front has a sign that says CHIEN MÉCHANT—"Mean Dog." I throw a wary glance across the yard.

"The dog," the guide assures me, "is dead."

She leads me through the gate, past the house, and into a garage whose floor is littered with dusty champagne bottles and elaborate metal contraptions used to insert corks. Then she flips on an electric lantern, and we descend a narrow spiral staircase some ninety feet into the ground. The temperature quickly drops from a dry, sunny 80 degrees to a brisk 45 degrees moistened by 90 percent humidity.[25]

The guide explains that the cellars are about one hundred and fifty years old; they served as part of a vast network of underground shelters during World War II. Patches of the brick walls still bear burns from candles used to light the corridors when electricity went out during air raids. I'm still mulling this fact when we arrive in a room glimmering with golden bottles of Armand de Brignac. They hang by the dozen in racks, slanted at a slight angle so that sediment collects in the necks and can be removed easily in the next step of the champagne-making process.

The spectacle of thousands of bottles sitting like gilded test tubes is quite impressive, but what really strikes me is that the bottles themselves are completely blank. There are no labels on the front or back, and nothing to distinguish a $300 bottle of Armand de Brignac from, say, a $60 bottle of Antique Gold, which Cattier stopped producing in 2006— the same year the house started producing Armand de Brignac. ("It's the old cuvée that's been sort of resurrected," a New York liquor store manager named J. J. Battipaglia would tell me upon my return to the States.[26])

After the tour is complete, my guide takes me back into the daylight and over to Cattier's headquarters for a meeting with the company's brass. First to greet me is Philippe Bienvenu, Armand de Brignac's commercial director.

"Bonjour, Zack!" he says cheerfully.

He introduces me to a few more Cattier employees, including the family's kindly patriarch Jean-Jacques Cattier and his son Alexandre (who enthusiastically informs me that his wife just gave birth to their first son, Armand). As we walk around the bright corridors of the Cattier headquarters, Bienvenu traces the origins of the company's flagship champagne to Jean-Jacques Cattier's mother, who first thought up the name in the early 1950s. "The name Armand de Brignac was created after the name of a book that Mrs. Cattier had read," he explains. "She really loved this character, she found the name very elegant, and this is how she decided to use the name to create that brand."[27]

The brand, which wasn't really even a brand at that point, remained dormant while Cattier focused on its existing brands like Antique Gold. According to Bienvenu, the house started to think about making Mrs. Cattier's idea a reality during the early 1990s, but nothing was officially done until fifteen years later. Shortly after Armand de Brignac's debut, Bienvenu claims, Jay-Z came across it purely by chance. "When we started to ship product to the U.S. and especially to New York, Jay discovered our champagne in a wine shop and bought a few bottles," he says. "There has never been any partnership, any financial involvement, or something like this between Jay and us . . . It's fantastic to have such an endorsement."

As I press Bienvenu for more details, the cracks in the story begin to show.

"How," I ask, "did the champagne find its way into Jay-Z's 'Show Me What You Got' video?"

"He discovered our champagne by pure coincidence in a wine shop and a few months after came to Monaco to shoot a video," Bienvenu replies. "On that occasion, he ordered a few cases that we shipped to his hotel there. We couldn't imagine when we shipped those cases that the purpose of this was to include our champagne in the video. We just thought that he wanted to enjoy our champagne during his stay in France."

I nod politely. But when I ask Bienvenu for the name of the New York wine shop in which Jay-Z allegedly found his first bottle of Armand de Brignac, the affable Frenchman quickly becomes defensive.

"I don't know which wine shop," he says. "I can't tell you any more details because I don't know."

All of this makes for a great story: a family-owned champagne brand dreamed up by a little old French lady in the 1950s, dormant until resurrected half a century later, promptly discovered by the world's most famous rapper, by sheer coincidence. Even more fantastic is the notion that Jay-Z—a man who'd launched his own Scottish vodka brand four years earlier, just so that he could rap about it—would decide, out of the kindness of his heart, to include the mom-and-pop champagne in the music video for the biggest single on his comeback album. It's about as believable as the notion that Jay-Z did his 2006 Budweiser commercial, carved from that same Monaco shoot, for free (in fact, a source tells me

Anheuser-Busch financed the whole shoot and paid him $1 million on top of that for his efforts).

The first bottles of Armand de Brignac weren't shipped until October 2006—months after Jay-Z's video was filmed. The U.S. Patent and Trademark Office confirms that the Armand de Brignac trademark was first used for commerce in November 2006.[28] Bienvenu himself admitted that the bottles were first shipped and released in the fall of 2006.[29] Obviously, it would have been impossible for Jay-Z to stumble upon a bottle of champagne in a New York wine shop during the preceding summer.

When I later confronted one of Cattier's publicists about this inconsistency, she backtracked. "There's a misunderstanding regarding how Jay saw the bottle. It was in New York . . . but not in a store," she explained in an e-mail. "Prior to the launch of Armand de Brignac, our U.S. importer was showing the brand to selected 'tastemakers' to generate excitement and spread word-of-mouth in key circles. . . . Through some of these connections, word reached someone in Jay's team of the brand and that's how his interest was sparked. Like any new brand coming to market, a number of key people would have seen it, tasted it, and learnt about it before it was released." Pressed on the nature of Jay-Z's connection to the importer, Sovereign Brands, she responded: "I know there have been some discussions between the two sides about potentially forming a relationship."[30]

In the weeks following my return from France, I realized that the answers to Jay-Z's champagne mystery were here in the U.S. all along. I spoke with a number of sources close to the matter—including a prominent executive at a major record label, a wine distributor with ties to the entertainment industry, and the chief executive of a notable liquor company, to name a few—and none of them would let me quote them by name for fear of damaging business relationships. But when I related everything I'd learned, all of these sources confirmed that Jay-Z receives millions of dollars per year for his association with Armand de Brignac. As I suspected, the connection wasn't through the Cattier family, but through Sovereign Brands.

Jay-Z and those around him publicly deny any connection to Armand de Brignac because he wants to be seen as a champagne connoisseur, a trendsetter with the sophistication to anoint a successor to Cristal as hip-hop's choice bubbly—not something as gauche as a paid promoter. Or, as Bienvenu offhandedly explained to me: "He doesn't want to be considered a brand ambassador or something like this." More important, Jay-Z realizes that the revelation of a financial connection could endanger the authenticity of his endorsement—and by extension jeopardize a very lucrative arrangement. Most of the people buying bottles of Armand de Brignac are doing so because they think Jay-Z prefers it to other fine wines simply because of its quality, much as he prefers Maybachs to Toyota Camrys. If they discovered that they were actually paying

$300 for a gussied-up bottle of $60 Antique Gold, they might reconsider.

The math looks extremely favorable for Jay-Z. Like most expensive champagnes, the production cost per bottle is about $13; the wholesale price is $225.[31] Armand de Brignac's maximum output is sixty thousand bottles per year.[32] If Jay-Z splits the $212-per-bottle profit evenly with Cattier and Sovereign, a back-of-the-envelope calculation suggests his annual take would be a little over $4 million. One of the industry sources who asked to remain anonymous confirmed that number, and added that Jay-Z may have received a Sovereign Brands equity stake worth about $50 million.[33] All for dropping a few lyrical references and featuring Armand de Brignac in a couple of videos.

"If he's not getting a cut, or if he doesn't own a piece, then he's not a good businessman," adds Fass. "And we all know Jay-Z is a good businessman."[34]

At least for now, Jay-Z gets to have his champagne—and drink it, too.

8

To Infinity–and Beyoncé

The rumors started swirling again on April Fools' Day, 2008. It was a delightfully confusing twist to the six-year saga of Jay-Z and Beyoncé Knowles's romance, which had endured dozens of erroneous reports of elopements and secret ceremonies. As the week wore on, though, it started to become clear that Jay-Z and Beyoncé were finally getting married.

Or were they? On April 1, *People* reported that the couple had secured a marriage license in the posh New York suburb of Scarsdale,[1] but other rumormongers remained skeptical. On the morning of April 4, Gawker weighed in with a story entitled "Beyoncé and Jay-Z Definitely, Maybe Getting Married Today." TMZ followed with another entitled "We Are Sooooo Not Buying It." But as the afternoon of April 4 unfolded, more details surfaced. Beyoncé's mother Tina was spotted in New York along with Beyoncé's former Destiny's Child group-mates Michelle Williams and Kelly Rowland. A white tent popped up on the rooftop terrace of Jay-Z's Tribeca penthouse. Someone photographed a set of candelabras sitting on the sidewalk in front of the building after being unloaded from a truck.[2]

Then the deluge began. At 5:47 P.M., Tina Knowles arrived. Twenty minutes later came Beyoncé's father, Mathew Knowles. At 6:27 P.M., Jay-Z's Maybach was spotted en route to the building. An hour later, actress Gwyneth Paltrow and rocker Chris Martin joined the other celebrities gathering at Jay-Z's apartment.[3] An insider let it slip that fifty thousand orchid blooms had been ordered for a "big party" at the mogul's pad. By the end of the night, the gossip hounds were in agreement: Jay-Z and Beyoncé had finally tied the knot. "It happened earlier this evening," a source informed *People*. "Jay wanted it to be a really private affair—close friends and family."[4]

Jay-Z and Beyoncé stayed mum on the details even after their wedding had been widely reported. The first official confirmation of the marriage came nearly three weeks later, when a Scarsdale town clerk confirmed that the court had received the signed license, which listed the wedding date as April 4.[5] It wasn't until September that Beyoncé finally showed off her $5 million Lorraine Schwartz wedding ring— an 18-carat flawless diamond set in a thin platinum band—a fittingly spectacular token to commemorate an alliance of seismic proportions.[6]

"In terms of the entertainment industry, it's the biggest merger you could possibly imagine," says music historian Jeff Chang. "It's two superpowers coming together. It's sort of Microsoft and Apple deciding they can be literally in bed together."[7]

The secrecy that preceded Jay-Z and Beyoncé's marriage is the by-product of what started out as an extremely unlikely union. In 2002, when the pair first became involved, Jay-Z wasn't the sophisticated mogul he is today. He possessed neither an Andy Warhol Rorschach-blot painting[8] nor a swank Tribeca penthouse in which to hang it. He favored do-rags and basketball jerseys over button-downs and slacks. He palled around with Damon Dash, Foxy Brown, and Beanie Sigel—not Gwyneth Paltrow, Chris Martin, and Oprah.

If you were to walk down 125th Street on a steamy summer day in 2002, you'd likely hear Jay-Z's "Girls, Girls, Girls" emanating from at least a few rolled-down car windows. You'd hear about all the women he was seeing, as well as the culinary perks of their ethnicities ("Spanish chick, French chick, Indian, and black / That's fried chicken, curry chicken, damn, I'm gettin' fat") and the raunchy ramifications of their professions ("I get frequent flyer mileage from my stewardess chick, she look right in that tight blue dress, she's thick / She gives me extra pillows and seat-back love, so I had to introduce her to the Mile High Club").[9]

Along with the abundance of Jay-Z's self-proclaimed

dalliances, there were plenty of other obstacles to a union with Beyoncé. Jay-Z got his first introduction to the business world by peddling crack on the streets. He narrowly avoided jail time for allegedly stabbing record producer Lance Rivera for bootlegging his songs; when Jay-Z met Beyoncé, he was still on probation. These aren't the sort of traits most young women look for, nor are they the type of qualities that tend to sit well with parents of twenty-year-olds—especially ones like Beyoncé's.

The superstar diva was raised as a devout Methodist by parents Mathew and Tina Knowles. (Tina's maiden name was Beyoncé, and she passed it along to her daughter so that it would continue on in another generation.[10]) Along with her younger sister, Solange, Beyoncé grew up in a four-bedroom mock-Tudor house in an upper-middle-class neighborhood of Houston, Texas. Her mother owned a hair salon; her father was a successful salesman at Xerox.[11] "I didn't grow up poor," Beyoncé explained to *Vanity Fair* in 2005. "I went to private school; we had a very nice house, cars, a housekeeper. I wasn't [singing] because I didn't have a choice, or to support the family, or because I had to get out of a bad situation. I just was determined; this is what I wanted to do so bad."[12]

Beyoncé got her start in entertainment as a first-grader, thanks to the keen eye of a dance teacher who noticed her and convinced her to enter the school's talent show. The spirited performer who emerged from the otherwise shy Beyoncé surprised even her parents. "The first time I saw her onstage at a school talent show, she was seven and just a different person," Mathew Knowles said in 2003. "Tina and I just looked at each other and said: 'Wow! Where did that come from?' "[13]

In 1990, at age nine, Beyoncé joined an R&B group called Girl's Tyme, which earned an appearance on the television show *Star Search* the following year. Despite a heart-breaking defeat on the *American Idol*-style program, Beyoncé was hooked on music, and so was her family. Her father left his job to manage his daughter's group and rechristened it Destiny's Child. At first, gigs were limited to practice at Tina's salon, where audiences were actually captive—women in curlers, immobilized by bonnet dryers.[14] During the summers, Mathew put together a sort of entertainment boot camp for the girls, complete with dance practice, vocal lessons, and a strict exercise regimen.[15]

In 1996, Destiny's Child scored a deal with Columbia records; the group's self-titled debut hit stores in 1998. Shortly after the release of a second album the following year, two of four members left the group and filed a lawsuit claiming that Mathew Knowles favored his daughter (the case was eventually settled). Beyoncé was crushed, admitting that she fell into a deep depression after the split. But the group quickly gained a new member and released the aptly named *Survivor* in 2001. The reincarnated Destiny's Child went on indefinite hiatus in 2002 before splitting amicably in 2004, giving Beyoncé the freedom to pursue a solo career.[16]

Throughout the many incarnations of Destiny's Child, bombshell Beyoncé remained shy offstage. When it came to dating, she claimed she was something of a wallflower. "I had a boyfriend from ninth grade until twelfth grade, the same guy," she told *Vanity Fair*. "I met him in church, and I went to his prom, but I preferred to be at home singing in front of a stereo—recording, making songs, listening to the music I grew up with . . . All I wanted to do was watch videos and write songs and perform."[17]

In the rare moments when it seemed Beyoncé was feeling too proud of herself, her mother was quick to admonish her—particularly, Beyoncé recalled, on one occasion when she was nineteen. "We were in the record store, my mom and dad were both there, and my song was playing, and I was feeling like hot stuff . . . There were some really cute guys in the store who were noticing me, and I was like, 'Oh, yeah! I'm hot!' And my mom said, 'I'm talking to you.' And I kept singing. And so she smacked me—slapped me in my face, so hard. And my dad said, 'What are you doing?' Because I didn't get spankings growing up. They didn't believe in that. My mom said, 'She thinks she's hot stuff 'cos her single is out. Nobody cares about that! You are still my child. I brought you into this world, I can take you out of it! Now go sit in the car.' But it was the best thing she could have ever done to me because for the first time I realized I was losing sight of what was important."[18]

These severe reminders seem to have had a major impact on the young Beyoncé. Even as she became an international icon as the star of Destiny's Child, she cultivated a modest image. In interviews, she opened up about insecurities that seemed more typical of a normal college-aged woman than a pop diva. "One day, I counted the blemishes on my face," she explained in 2001. "Got up to thirty-five. It's so irritating to read in articles people saying, 'She thinks she's beautiful.' There's a lot of days when I wake up and hate how I look. . . . When I was little, my head was smaller, and I looked like I had big Dumbo ears. I still do not wear my ears out, and that's why I wear big earrings, because they camouflage your ears."[19]

It wasn't just Beyoncé who was dealing with a very human set of insecurities. According to Jay-Z's longtime mentor Jonathan "Jaz-O" Burks, the rapper sometimes struggled with issues of self-image. "He felt he needed money because he didn't feel like he was the most attractive guy to girls," says Jaz-O. "I think he had a serious complex about his features."[20] Regardless, Jay-Z did his best to project an air of invincibility. In his 2000 hit "Big Pimpin'," he laid out his romantic philosophy: "Me give my heart to a woman? Not for nothin', never happen / I'll be forever mackin'."[21]

At least that's what he wanted his audience to think. Chenise Wilson, a friend of Jay-Z and Damon Dash who spent a lot of time with both men in the early and late 1990s, paints a slightly different picture of Jay-Z's love life. "There were girls around, but that wasn't his thing, being in girls' faces," says Wilson. "He had his share, but he wasn't the kind of guy with a whole lot of girls. . . . I've heard stories that he's always had a girl and another girl and another girl. But, you know, those are stories. Jay is a very particular guy."[22]

Meanwhile, Beyoncé claimed she had trouble finding men. "I am trying to date, but there's no one special," she said in July 2002. "The crazy thing is that everyone tries to hook me up with somebody. I'm scared, and I didn't want to go out with anyone for a long time. I was always worried the tabloids would get a picture. Plus, I'm not a dating-type person."[23] Her shy-girl image might not have been completely representative of real life. New York papers linked her to controversial rapper Eminem in 2001[24] and suave super-producer Pharrell Williams in 2002.[25] "She ain't been a choir church girl since she left the church," says Wilson. "She was very skilled at keeping it quiet. I think it was a mutual thing with whoever she was involved with."

In any event, Jay-Z and Beyoncé hit it off while collaborating on the song "'03 Bonnie & Clyde" in early 2002. They'd known each other through the celebrity circuit, and Jay-Z approached Beyoncé about working together ostensibly because she was the most talented performer he knew. "I wanted a singer on the song," he said, "and I knew one who was exceptional." The song appeared on Jay-Z's seventh album, *The Blueprint 2: The Gift & The Curse*, and on international editions of Beyoncé's solo debut, *Dangerously in Love*, each of which sold more than three million copies.[26]

In July 2002, Beyoncé gave *Newsweek* a nondenial when asked about photos of her embracing the rapper. "We're good friends," she said. "To get a boyfriend, I have to date, and it's so hard to trust people. But I'm hopeful."[27] Jay-Z had similar concerns with trust. By his own admission, his issues were fostered by the trauma of being abandoned by his father as a preteen. "It [affected] my relationships with women," he told *Rolling Stone* in a 2005 interview. "I was always guarded, always guarded. And always suspicious. I never let myself just go."[28]

But after the music video for "'03 Bonnie and Clyde" came out in 2003, even casual observers could see that Jay-Z was beginning to let Beyoncé into his life in a meaningful way. In the video, Jay-Z and Beyoncé cruise the sepia sands of Mexico in a gunmetal gray Aston Martin. Unlike legendary outlaws Bonnie Parker and Clyde Barrow, they aren't robbing banks or sticking up gas stations (though the ever-present cash-filled duffel bag implies something of that ilk). Instead, they're seen cleverly evading the authorities through a series of maneuvers that would make James Bond proud, culminating in a scene where Jay-Z tosses his Aston Martin keys to a gas station attendant who's later stopped by the authorities as Jay-Z and Beyoncé ride off into the sunset in an old pickup truck.

Throughout the video, the choreography suggests a relationship beyond the screen. In the chorus, Jay-Z wraps his arm around Beyoncé while saying, "All I need in this life of sin / Is me and my girlfriend." Beyoncé replies, "Down to ride to the very end / Is me and my boyfriend." Appearing as even a fictional partner in crime was a departure for the clean-cut Beyoncé; similarly, being seen with a presumably devout pop diva was unusual for Jay-Z. Each brought the other a bit of something they didn't have before—and the collaboration marked the beginning of a symbiotic relationship inside and outside of the recording booth. "We exchanged audiences," Jay-Z said two years later. "Her records are huge Top 40 records, and she helped 'Bonnie and Clyde' go to number one. What I gave her was a street credibility, a different edge."[29]

Meanwhile, the back pages buzzed with speculation on Jay-Z and Beyoncé's relationship. In March 2003, papers in New York and Miami reported that the couple was already on the outs. "It sounds as though the music has stopped playing for Jay-Z and Beyoncé Knowles," crowed the *Miami Herald*. Reporters from New York's *Daily News* spotted the rapper with another woman at a Big Apple nightclub. Days later, the *Herald* quoted him talking about the video for "'03 Bonnie and Clyde" with a "wistful" air. "That's an old video," he said. "I've got a new video out."[30]

By the time Beyoncé released her solo debut *Dangerously in Love* in the summer of 2003, however, there was no doubt that Jay-Z and Beyoncé were a couple. The album's lead track was "Crazy in Love," a bombastic orgy of horns, bass, and cowbell, topped off with a verse from Jay-Z. The song went on to win two Grammy awards and countless other accolades, including a number three ranking on *Rolling Stone*'s list of the decade's best songs—right behind Jay-Z's "99 Problems," released later that same year.[31]

The song was also turned into an award-winning music

video. The final scene—Jay-Z and Beyoncé dancing together after setting fire to a nearby car—cemented the couple's status in the popular eye. Beyoncé also showcased her considerable dancing and rump-shaking abilities (toward the end of the clip, she kicks off the top of a fire hydrant and undulates in the resulting deluge for the balance of the video), but insisted that her increasingly sexy videos were still congruent with her religious views. "God is the main person in my life, and I would never do anything to offend Him," she told Britain's *Daily Mirror* in 2003. "I honestly believe He wants people to celebrate their bodies, as long as you don't compromise your Christianity in the process."[32]

Perhaps with this in mind, her replies to questions about Jay-Z were extremely limited early on in their relationship. When a *Vanity Fair* writer asked Beyoncé in 2005 if the sentiments she expressed in "Crazy in Love" were reflective of her feelings for Jay-Z, all she offered was, "Yes, it was very real."[33] As the years went on, Beyoncé elaborated a bit but remained stingy with details. "Most of [my] love songs are really personal," she explained in 2009. "I am so private always, it's like therapy for me to be able to sing about what I really care about, to release that."[34]

Songwriter and Beyoncé collaborator Amanda Ghost gave a more detailed explanation. "She keeps the Jay-Z references ambiguous, but music is the one place she can be incredibly expressive—look at the lyrics to the track 'Ave Maria,'" Ghost said in 2009. "She talks about being surrounded by friends, but she's alone: 'How can the silence seem so loud?'

and then, 'There's only us when the lights go down.' I think that's probably the most personal line on the whole album about her and Jay, because they are very real, and they're very much in love, and it must be pretty tough to have that love when you're incredibly famous."[35]

Beyoncé's attitude toward her fame, along with Jay-Z's obvious dedication to her, helped sell her parents on the notion of their daughter dating a former drug dealer. The more they got to know Jay-Z, the more they approved of him. "Jay is just such a gentleman, and he is so smart, I was so happy that they got together," Tina Knowles said in 2005. "They're two smart people, and it's great for both of them—it's such a great match."[36]

Following the success of "Crazy in Love" and the accompanying video, there has been nary a peep of bad news reported in Jay-Z and Beyoncé's relationship. "Jay and I have always been very private about our relationships," she told Larry King in 2009. "Even after we became husband and wife, we still continue to be private. And I think it's protected us from a lot of things. And people give us a lot of respect. And I guess I learned that as happy as I am, I still need to keep it private."[37]

Lacey Rose, the writer who penned Beyoncé's *Forbes* cover story in 2006, credits the couple's approach. "They're very tight-lipped about that relationship, and frankly, I think that's very wise," says Rose. "Their careers and products garner so much attention, they don't need their private lives to do that. That's what sets them apart from the celebrities lining the pages of *Us Weekly*. For many, it's their latest relationship drama that keeps them in the news. In the case of Jay-Z and Beyoncé, it's a concert or a video. That's not to say that their relationship isn't part of the tabloid culture, but they don't need to provide the details to stay relevant."[38]

Another reason Jay-Z and Beyoncé have largely avoided tabloid drama is that they're capable of turning off their stage personas, and often do. "Shawn Carter is happy to put on his Jay-Z suit, but then he goes back to being Mr. Carter," says entertainment lawyer Bernie Resnick in a telephone interview. "Most people think of him as a brash, big-shot guy. He's not. He's quiet, introspective. The guy wears nice clothes, nothing flashy. He's a gentleman." In person, Resnick says they're both very down-to-earth. "They're Mr. and Mrs. Carter going to dinner."[39]

Observers also note the sense of intimacy that Jay-Z and Beyoncé exude in person, very different from the unsentimental attitude with which Jay-Z approaches his business ventures. "They're careful to not be demonstrative in public, but spend some time around them and you'll see all the hallmarks of a close, committed couple," wrote Touré, in *Rolling Stone*'s 2005 cover story on Jay-Z. "They're physically playful, they eat oxtail off the same plate, she's often giggling at something he's said, they can talk with just their eyes."[40] Adds Jeff Chang: "It's the closest thing to love that we have in America, this marriage."[41]

Legitimacy of their love aside, the marriage makes both Jay-Z and Beyoncé even more attractive to advertisers. Though they've never endorsed a product together, a commercial appearance by one suggests the approval of the other. If Beyoncé shows up on TV enjoying a Pepsi, there's at least a subliminal suggestion that Jay-Z likes it, too, and vice versa. "If you get one, you're getting the other," says Chang. "It's an amazingly powerful situation that they have."[42] Adds media buyer Ryan Schinman: "It's a case of one plus one equals ten."[43]

The value of synergy isn't lost on the lovebirds. Both make note of it in Beyoncé's 2006 song "Upgrade U," which begins with a challenge from Jay-Z. "How you going to upgrade me? What's higher than number one?" Beyoncé returns by name-checking Ralph Lauren Purple Label neckties and Audemars Piguet watches, presumably brands he wouldn't have heard of were it not for her feminine sophistication. More interestingly, she outlines how she'll help him earn more money. "I'ma help you build your account," she says. "When you're in the big meetings for the mil[ions], you take me in just to complement the deal / Anything you cop I split the bill. Believe me, I can upgrade you."[44]

Whether Beyoncé is actually in the room when Jay-Z closes his deals, her tacit approval certainly is. That's something that can open doors that might previously have been closed. For example, in 2004—after Jay-Z and Beyoncé's relationship became common knowledge—Jay-Z purchased a seven-figure stake in Carol's Daughter, which makes skin and hair-care products for women and girls.[45] The move, which could be worth millions more as Carol's Daughter continues to grow, probably wouldn't have been possible if Jay-Z had still been "Big Pimpin'" when the opportunity arose.

Jay-Z and Beyoncé seem to be excellent role models for each other, career-wise. "I think they both recognize the value of branding themselves, and it's something they've both done really well," says Rose. "Both of them are people who recognize the key to being an entertainment mogul today is that you have to be everywhere. You can't just have an album or a clothing line or a movie, you have to have all those things. They're very good at that, and I'm sure it's a product of one inspiring the other."[46] Beyoncé's relentless appetite for touring, acting, recording, and anything else that can help her add to her own entertainment empire is another plus. "This is a girl that never, ever stops," says Rose. "Sleep doesn't seem to be a priority. That has to be inspiring for her husband." Sure enough, marrying Beyoncé brought a new meaning to the word *hustle* for Jay-Z. In the two years following their nuptials, the highlights of his frenetic schedule included recording his eleventh solo album, embarking on a world tour with stops in over fifty cities, and inking a ten-year, $150-million deal with concert promoter Live Nation.

Clearly, Jay-Z and Beyoncé haven't allowed marriage to get in the way of their rigorous touring and recording schedules. Being able to afford private jets is helpful, but even when they're on the road to see each other perform in concert, work comes first. On one occasion in early 2008, Beyoncé flew to Miami for a Jay-Z show but made sure to schedule some time in the recording studio beforehand with James "Jim Jonsin" Scheffer, a Grammy-winning producer based in South Florida.

"Beyoncé was coming into Miami to just listen to some music and meet us," Jonsin explains at an interview atop a Hollywood hotel on the eve of the 2010 Grammy awards. "It was this whole process, you had to meet the A&R [artists and repertoire specialist], you had to meet her father. It was almost a big background-check thing."[47]

Beyoncé's usual quality control measures were put into effect despite the fact that her sister, singer Solange, was the one who recommended Jonsin. Once he was cleared, Beyoncé set up a time to come to Jonsin's studio and listen to a few tracks he'd cooked up, including the one that eventually became "Sweet Dreams," a hit single. "We made the track, and she comes by around four or five o'clock to listen to it; she's going to go to Jay-Z's concert at six," recalls Jonsin. "So we play some music for her. That particular song, she went nuts. She loved it. She insisted on going in the vocal booth and recording it right then and there, so she started cutting it, and she was late to Jay-Z's concert."

Jonsin wasn't surprised. "I think their careers blossomed together," he says. "They're the president and first lady of the music industry, they run shit . . . By marrying Beyoncé, he attached himself to all her fans, and then they went and got into his stuff. The same goes for her, she got a bunch of new fans from him."

As much as they gained from their marriage, Jay-Z and Beyoncé stand to raise their profiles even further once they start a family of their own. "For both of them, it adds another dimension," says Rose. "From a promotion or endorsement standpoint, it adds another audience. For an output stand-point for Beyoncé, obviously she won't be able to do one hundred and fifty tour dates per year anymore, so maybe it's Broadway. This is not a woman who's going to slow down."[48] And for Jay-Z, becoming a father will further improve his endorsement prospects. "Now he becomes a family man, and he opens up to a different world, a different side of the business," says Schinman. "If you see what's going on right now, family sells. I think he's got nothing but upside."[49]

So in the end, is the union of Jay-Z and Beyoncé a marriage or a merger? Listen to the song "Upgrade U," released barely a year before the pair got hitched, for the answer. Toward the middle of Jay-Z's verse, he mentions that Beyoncé is "on the verge" of something that rhymes with "verge." But the word—either "marriage" or "merge"—is slurred. For a rhymester as precise as Jay-Z, that's likely no accident: his relationship with Beyoncé is both.

Net Gain

On a bright and bitter day in March 2009, a clump of New York's most influential citizens has clustered around the site of the billion-dollar Barclays Center, future home of the NBA's Brooklyn Nets. Backed by a yellow Caterpillar excavator, the distinguished crew includes Mayor Michael Bloomberg, Governor David Paterson, and Borough President Marty Markowitz, all clad in dark suits and hard hats, shovels ready to kick off a symbolic groundbreaking.

The eyes of the ceremony's onlookers, however, aren't focused on any of the politicians. They're directed toward the man towering at least a foot above the diminutive Markowitz: Jay-Z, co-owner of the Nets, and looking the part in a three-piece suit over a Gordon Gekko–style white-collared shirt. Suddenly, a loud pop echoes through the cold air and a stream of blue confetti rains down. Jay-Z and the politicians dip their shovels into the dirt as cameras click.

Later that day, local officials gather to puff their political feathers at a press conference in the shelter of an enormous tent. The Barclays Center is back on track after years of delays and lawsuits, soon to rise as the centerpiece of the ambitious Atlantic Yards development to be built atop the rail yard of the same name. After perhaps one too many jokes about Beyoncé, Markowitz introduces Jay-Z, and the mogul strides to the podium.

"What I stand here and represent is hope for Brooklyn, New York City," says Jay-Z, after the initial applause dies down. "I think about growing up in Brooklyn in Marcy projects and shooting jump shots thinking I could make it to the NBA. Now I'm standing here as an owner of a team that's coming back to Brooklyn and [taking] pride in that, in bringing that dream so much closer."

Just fifteen years before becoming the target of Marty Markowitz's chummy wisecrackery at the future site of the Barclays Center, Jay-Z's business in Brooklyn was of the illegal variety. The same impulse that led him into that line of work—an unquenchable thirst for wealth and a flair for deal-making—drew Jay-Z into the business of basketball. The Nets' move from New Jersey to Brooklyn was possible only after years of wrangling at the highest levels of government and business. Through it all, Jay-Z maneuvered himself into a position to both bring NBA basketball to his hometown and squeeze every dollar he could out of the equation.

The connection between Jay-Z and the Nets began with a half-serious suggestion from star point guard Jason Kidd in 2003. Kidd was hosting a birthday party at Jay-Z's 40/40 Club and joked that the rapper ought to buy a stake in the Nets. The idea intrigued Jay-Z, and that fall he met with real estate developer Bruce Ratner, one of four bidders attempting to buy the team. Unlike the other bidders, Ratner's ultimate goal was to move the team to Brooklyn, where he'd erect a sparkling new arena and surround it with high-rise commercial and residential towers.[1]

The plot of land Ratner coveted was an oddly shaped triangle above the rail yards at the intersection of Atlantic and Flatbush avenues at the edge of downtown Brooklyn. A half-century earlier, Brooklyn Dodgers owner Walter O'Malley had hoped to build a new home for his team on the same site. (O'Malley eventually moved the team to Los Angeles when Robert Moses, who wanted a stadium in Queens, repeatedly blocked him from acquiring the land.[2]) Ratner was hoping to do what O'Malley couldn't: convince the city to use eminent domain laws to help him clear the additional acreage needed for his development.

Ratner's plan was not an easy one to execute. To win his bid for the Nets, he would have to come up with the most lucrative package and also secure the Brooklyn stadium site. To secure the stadium site, he would have to woo city officials by proving there was enough support for the project from

Brooklyn's constituents to overcome the powerful group of mostly upper-middle-class residents opposed to the construction of a giant entertainment complex in the middle of their neighborhood. Enter Jay-Z, one of the borough's most popular sons.

In December of 2003, Jay-Z joined a team of would-be investors in Ratner's consortium to unveil plans for a billowy silver stadium designed by architect Frank Gehry. The arena would be surrounded by four high-rise towers with 2.1 million square feet of space, along with 4,500 new apartments to the east, all part of Ratner's $2.5 billion project. The entire development would be easily accessible to the nearby Atlantic Terminal, home to nine subway lines and a major commuter railroad station. After Jay-Z's appearance and Gehry's plans drummed up support for the proposal, New Jersey governor Jim McGreevey attempted to one-up Ratner by announcing he'd secured $150 million from his state to build a rail line to the Nets' old home in East Rutherford.[3] At that point, Ratner's $275 million bid for the Nets was the highest on the table, though other bidders publicly questioned his ability to see such an outlandish plan through to completion. Amid these concerns and rumblings that a New Jersey–based group was preparing to up its bid, Ratner increased his offer to $300 million. In late January of 2004, the offer submitted by Ratner and his consortium of investors was accepted. The Nets were coming to Brooklyn.[4]

As soon as the deal closed, Jay-Z became a co-owner of the Nets, making him one of the few artists to hold an ownership stake in a major professional sports franchise. "It all came together in some weird way," he said. "I still didn't believe it happened even as I was signing the contract to be a part of the ownership. I was like, 'What is this? Is this real?' It was just so surreal. I still can't believe when I say it."[5]

Jay-Z shrewdly entered into negotiations at a time when Ratner was desperate for a big splash to help his project overcome major political obstacles. Both knew that Jay-Z's popularity could help the plans for a new arena gain momentum. "From the standpoint of political lobbying, having somebody of that celebrity value can be a difference maker," says Paul Swangard, director of the University of Oregon's Warsaw Sports Marketing Center. "Certainly a portion of the district in that area would be fans of Jay-Z, and if he were to endorse an issue that has some pretty big political ramifications, I think the political value of him being involved in this process is pretty substantial."[6] In addition, the rapper brought the Nets a glamour previously reserved for the team's cross-river rival. If Jay-Z was able to launch his wildly successful S. Carter sneaker in partnership with Reebok—and not Nike—surely he could lend the same credibility to the Nets, who'd long taken a backseat to the New York Knicks. "People grew up on the Knicks," Jay-Z explained. "The Nets have always been the cousins. I hope to change that."[7]

Jay-Z also had the potential to directly affect the makeup of the Nets through his relationship with one of basketball's biggest stars: LeBron James. The two men became close during the summer of 2003, when James joined Jay-Z's Entertainers

Basketball Classic street basketball team. After evening games under the lights at Rucker Park in Harlem, James and the other players would head downtown to carouse their nights away as the guests of honor at Jay-Z's brand-new 40/40 Club alongside the likes of Sean "Diddy" Combs and Beyoncé Knowles. Though James signed his rookie contract with the Cleveland Cavaliers that same year, his star-spangled summer certainly gave him a taste of what it might be like to play in New York. Ratner likely realized that James's first contract expired at the end of the 2006–2007 season—right around the time the Brooklyn arena was initially scheduled to open[8]— and that Jay-Z might be able to help persuade the young star to become the centerpiece of the rejuvenated franchise.

Having Jay-Z on board boosted the Nets' chances of successfully moving to Brooklyn, winning over Knicks fans, and landing LeBron James. The rapper knew how to leverage this reality. Details of Jay-Z's stake in the Nets were never officially disclosed, but New York newspapers did their requisite digging and came up with some numbers. The *Daily News* reported that Jay-Z invested $1 million in the team,[9] while the *Post* pegged his holdings at 1.5 percent.[10] The latter figure would put the value of Jay-Z's stake in the $300 million team at $4.5 million. Though the two reports seem to contradict each other at first glance, they both make sense under one scenario: that Jay-Z invested $1 million and received a 1.5 percent stake worth $4.5 million, demanding a deep discount on his purchase because of everything that both he and Ratner knew he'd bring to the Nets.

Publicly, Jay-Z disputes this notion. "Nobody gave me anything," he declared in 2005. "I spent my money like everyone else, and I came in and added value."[11] The semantics of this statement are a bit tricky. It's easy enough to believe that he didn't get his stake for free, but just because he spent money doesn't mean he didn't get a discount. Celebrities often get sweetheart deals when buying stakes in professional sports teams, and failing to take advantage of an option like that just doesn't fit with Jay-Z's ruthless business instincts. "These deals can vary wildly in terms of celebrities paying full freight or not," explains Kurt Badenhausen, a *Forbes* senior editor who specializes in team valuations. "Whether a celebrity is receiving some sort of perks or reciprocal arrangements, they sometimes get a discount on what a nonfamous investor might pay for their stake."[12]

In any case, Jay-Z wasn't getting only a discounted rate. He was getting a discounted rate on an asset that was sure to dramatically increase in value with a move to Brooklyn. Badenhausen estimates that the Nets will be worth about $500 million once ensconced in the Barclays Center, nearly twice what the team was worth in New Jersey. When Jay-Z first bought into the team, he undoubtedly realized that his $1 million investment, already worth $4.5 million, was bound to swell to nearly $8 million within a matter of years. In effect, he received a virtually guaranteed eight-fold return on investment just for attaching his name to the Nets, plus a potential share of the hefty operating income thrown off by a successful basketball team in the nation's largest market.

≡

Jay-Z stood to gain millions from his investment in the Nets, but his presence proved to be a boost to the team as well. A year after the sale was finalized, Ratner declared Jay-Z one of his five most active owners. In addition to consulting with Ratner and Nets CEO Brett Yormark on marketing issues and stadium design plans, the rapper released a Nets-themed remix of his song "Takeover" during the team's 2005 playoff run. He and Beyoncé immediately became a courtside fixture at the Nets' otherwise unsexy home games in the swamps of eastern New Jersey.[13]

Jay-Z struck up a relationship with Frank Gehry shortly after both joined Ratner's group. The physical evidence could be seen at Jay-Z's old Def Jam office, where a two-foot-tall 3-D model of Gehry's Atlantic Yards plan sat on a table, right beneath a picture of Jay-Z schmoozing with Prince Charles in London. Gehry also suggested to Jay-Z that James Joyce was the first rapper. "When I listen to the tapes of his voice doing *Finnegans Wake*, it sounds like rap," Gehry noted. "He's very fast with the Irish accent, it's all slurred together, and it's quite interesting. When I heard it I thought he was a rapper, and I sent them to Jay-Z because I thought he might like it." (When Gehry mailed Jay-Z a heap of Joyce novels, the rapper politely explained that he reads only nonfiction.)[14]

In his first summer as part-owner, Jay-Z flashed his

talents as a recruiter. The Nets' then-coach Lawrence Frank asked him to call All-Star Shareef Abdur-Rahim and sell the forward on coming to the Nets. Whatever Jay-Z said to him worked, and the Portland Trailblazers agreed to the parameters of a sign-and-trade deal. Though the agreement eventually fell through when a medical exam revealed issues with Abdur-Rahim's knee,[15] the episode gave Ratner a tantalizing taste of Jay-Z's ability to persuade players to join the team—perhaps, someday, the mighty LeBron James.

James wouldn't become a free agent for years, but in the meantime, Ratner was growing increasingly appreciative of Jay-Z and everything he brought to the Nets, though he'd take a bit more time to warm up to the rapper's music. "Someone in my office gave me the lyrics to one of his rap songs off the Internet and I said, 'Oh my God,'" Ratner told the *Daily News*. "[But] any preconceived notion I had about rap artists—the lyrics made me wonder—changed . . . You could see right away, you spend ten minutes with [Jay-Z], he is a soft-spoken, mild-mannered, intelligent guy who really knows what is going on."[16]

Once the initial excitement over the Nets' future dwindled, Ratner and Jay-Z began to face the reality of the team's uncertain intermediate fate. With an eye toward their Brooklyn debut, the Nets traded star forward Kenyon Martin for three first-round draft picks in 2004. Already miffed by the team's impending move, New Jersey fans stopped showing up to home games. As attendance declined, the Nets traded away more of their stars, and the cycle continued. Not even

Jay-Z's frequent courtside appearances and lyrical references ("Now we own a ball team, holla back!") could generate enough excitement to keep people coming to the arena. Jason Kidd, the player who'd first suggested Jay-Z invest in the team, was sent packing in 2008. LeBron James signed a contract extension with the Cavaliers that kept him in Cleveland through the end of the 2009–2010 season, by which point the Nets were struggling to draw one thousand people to games at the nineteen-thousand-seat Izod Center. The team finished the campaign with an abysmal record of twelve wins and seventy losses and ranked last among all NBA teams in attendance.[17]

Meanwhile, the scheduled 2008 groundbreaking date for the Nets' new Brooklyn home had long since passed. Ratner's plan was bogged down with lawsuits from angry residents, including a group called Develop—Don't Destroy Brooklyn. By the time legal challenges filed against the development stalled the arena's construction, Ratner's crews had already knocked down twenty-six buildings. While lawyers battled over the project's fate, the gash in the neighborhood's urban fabric lingered, further angering residents.[18]

Though the Nets secured a twenty-year, $400-million naming rights deal with Barclays in 2007, the following year's recession came at the worst possible time for Ratner's group. The Nets were now losing about $25 million to $30 million per year in New Jersey, and Atlantic Yards's construction costs had doubled to nearly $1 billion. If Ratner couldn't scare up the financing for the arena, he risked losing the rights to develop the property.

"I would bet if you started back in '03 and somebody told him how long this would be and how expensive the fight would be, his stockholders, partners, whatever they are, and even probably him, would say, 'You know, if you really costed it all out, you won't make money and you shouldn't do it,'" Mayor Bloomberg told the *Wall Street Journal* in 2010. "He's had some very difficult times. He's had to invest an awful lot more at less desirable terms than what the original business model said."[19]

To save his project, Ratner had to make some major concessions. Given the ballooning costs of Atlantic Yards and relative lack of financing available, he decided to abandon Gehry's extravagant plan and shift to a scaled-back version. He also reworked his agreement with New York's Metropolitan Transit Authority, replacing the scheduled $100 million purchase of the Atlantic Yards site with a series of payments that would cost him more over time. By 2009, he still faced a $300 million financing gap at a time when credit was scarce and investors scarcer. Ratner needed somebody even wealthier than Jay-Z, and fortunately he found one: Russian billionaire Mikhail Prokhorov.

An eccentric six-foot-eight-inch metals baron, Prokhorov spent his leisure time kickboxing and buying up distressed assets—like the Nets—with the $10 billion fortune he'd amassed by 2009.[20] That July, he met with Ratner to discuss the possibility of buying the team. Within two weeks, the pair had settled on the outlines of the deal, which was finalized nearly a year later. The arrangement called for

Prokhorov to pay $200 million for an 80 percent stake in the Nets, a 45 percent share of the stadium, and an option to buy 20 percent of the surrounding real estate projects that Ratner would stay on to develop.[21] Part of the reason Prokhorov was so eager to become majority owner of the Nets was the opportunity to partner with Jay-Z. Shortly after finalizing his purchase, the mining tycoon met Jay-Z and said he felt lucky to be working with him. "Despite the fact that I am very far from the rap music, we have a lot in common," he said. "I share his passion for Brooklyn."[22]

Prokhorov also knew of Jay-Z's value as a recruiter heading into the summer of 2010, when arguably the best crop of free agents in NBA history would become available. The class included guard Dwyane Wade, the league's 2008–2009 scoring champ, as well as power forwards Chris Bosh and Amar'e Stoudemire, both five-time All-Stars. The ultimate prize, however, was LeBron James. Just twenty-five years old, he was entering that golden moment of an athlete's career where a lack of experience no longer inhibits performance and age hasn't yet begun to do so. During the 2009–2010 season, James averaged nearly thirty points per game and led the Cavaliers to the best record in the Eastern Conference for the second year in a row. Without a strong cast of players around him, however, he was unable to carry his team to the finals; the Cavaliers fell to the Boston Celtics in the semifinal round of the NBA playoffs.

Teams were allowed to start negotiating with players on July 1, 2010, but the frenzy began well before the first day of free agency. In Cleveland, a host of local personalities got together to record a video entitled "We Are LeBron," while fans in Los Angeles planned a parade in James's honor. Even Mayor Bloomberg weighed in. "LeBron James would love living in New York," he said. "It is the world's greatest stage."[23] The teams themselves had started preparing for the LeBron sweepstakes years in advance. Both the Nets and the Knicks had cleared enough room under the NBA's salary cap to offer two league-maximum contracts. The Miami Heat, Chicago Bulls, and Los Angeles Clippers also had the ability to sign James to a maximum deal and bring in another high-profile free agent to play alongside him. James's hometown Cavaliers, meanwhile, didn't have the cap space to bring in another star, but NBA rules allowed them to offer James a more lucrative contract than any other team.

Though Mikhail Prokhorov was the newcomer at this particular party, he was quick to give the basketball world—especially the Knicks—a taste of Russian diplomacy. Just days before the free agent signing period began, Prokhorov commissioned a 225-foot-tall mural across the street from Madison Square Garden. The advertisement featured the billionaire standing side-by-side with Jay-Z, with the motto "The Blueprint for Greatness" emblazoned above.[24] "I think Jay and I look really great, and I am looking into the possibility of buying this building and having it shipped back to Moscow," Prokhorov quipped. "I want to put it across the Red Square near the Kremlin."[25]

Days later, the Nets showed up their rivals once again.

LeBron James invited Prokhorov and Jay-Z to Cleveland to court him first, before Knicks owner James Dolan and his crew. When reporters following Dolan's car caught sight of the Nets' delegation, they abandoned Dolan and chased after Prokhorov and Jay-Z. The day's events prompted New York's *Daily News* to declare that Dolan was "playing second-fiddle to his cross-river rivals."[26] It seemed the Nets were no longer the cousins.

During the following week, the LeBron James story exploded into a national obsession. Though the Nets may have appeared to be his most likely destination on day one, the following day's reports had him going to Chicago; after that, Miami, with sports media outlets across the country weighing in on every rumor. When James scheduled a press conference for July 8 in Greenwich, Connecticut, the focus briefly shifted back to the Knicks. On Wall Street, trading of Madison Square Garden, Inc. stock options surged to a record high.[27]

By the time James arrived in Greenwich to announce his decision, fans across the country were in hysterics. Millions tuned in to ESPN's exclusive broadcast at 9 p.m. Eastern Time to watch the drama unfold. After nearly a half hour of beating around the proverbial bush, James revealed his plans. "This fall," he said nervously, "I'm going to take my talents to South Beach and join the Miami Heat." When asked why he made his choice, he responded, "I think the major factor, the major reason, in my decision was the best opportunity to win, and to win now and to win into the future."[28]

Indeed, heading to Miami offered James the best chance to win—he made his decision after the summer's two other premier free agents, Dwyane Wade and Chris Bosh, signed with the Heat. While Jay-Z and Prokhorov were disappointed, it was clear that Miami offered something they couldn't. Wisely, they refused to drown their sorrows by signing second-tier free agents to maximum contracts, as pundits suggested the Knicks did by signing Stoudemire. "We put on the list three top players," said Prokhorov. "They had the decision to move to Miami. As far as other top players are concerned, they are really good, but we didn't plan to put them on the roster because they are very good, but not good enough to make a championship for our team. . . . Be patient. . . . Support our team. We will win for sure."[29]

Prokhorov, Jay-Z, and the Nets may have missed out on the prize of the 2009–2010 free agent class, but they forced their way into the conversation for the first time in years. As the move to Brooklyn draws nearer, the team's appeal will only increase—thanks to the prospect of rising ticket sales and concession stand revenues—as will the value of Jay-Z's $1 million investment. Already worth $4.5 million, it could rise well beyond the $8 million predicted earlier in this chapter if the Nets' young core of players develops into a cast of All-Stars, or if the team lands one of the marquee free agents set to hit the market in coming years.

Pleasant as those options sound, there's still a chance that the Nets' grandest plan may yet work. LeBron James's contract with the Miami Heat includes an escape clause that would allow him to become a free agent again in 2014,[30] shortly after the Nets move to Brooklyn. Once the new arena is complete, Jay-Z might have more luck convincing his pal to switch sides—and at least one prominent Brooklynite believes that's exactly what will happen.

"LeBron James has worked hard in Cleveland," explained Borough President Markowitz the day after James signed with Miami. "So maybe he needs this vacation in Florida before he moves on to reach his professional zenith—a championship dynasty in Brooklyn."[31]

10

Who Killed the Jay-Z Jeep?

On a lazy Monday morning a few days before Christmas, I'm on the phone with Detroit-based marketing guru Michael Berrin, and I'm beginning to think I need another cup of coffee. In a prior life, Berrin performed as rapper MC Serch; friends still call him Serch. He's known Jay-Z since the mogul was a lanky teenager rapping for room and board on Big Daddy Kane's tour bus. Thus far in our conversation, Serch, who admits he's prone to going off on tangents, is mostly telling tales about hip-hop in the late 1980s and how fantastic it was to rap with Tupac Shakur before he was famous. The stories are fascinating, but I'm beginning to wonder if I'll hear anything about Jay-Z and his business savvy.

After Serch pauses to thank his wife for picking up bagels, the conversation shifts to the auto industry. He launches into a diatribe about what's wrong with Detroit—an ambitious topic for an hour-long conversation—and my eyes drift away from my computer screen toward the window. My fire escape is barely visible beneath a foot of snow, still plump and pale three days after a blizzard blew through New York. I briefly feel myself starting to reconsider global warming. Suddenly, Serch mentions Jay-Z's name, snapping me from my reverie.

"That deal was the most fucked-up deal that I've ever seen or heard of," he says. "I came to Jay with the automobile industry in my back pocket to do a Shawn Carter edition vehicle that he approved, only to have the automobile industry basically shoot it down for fear that he was a bigger star than the car."

Just as he's about to elaborate on his point, Serch is interrupted by the blare of a cell phone (the ringtone, fittingly, is Jay-Z's "Empire State of Mind"). He quickly turns off the phone and apologizes. When I press him for more details about the Jay-Z vehicle, he tells me that it was going to be a "Jay-Z Jeep" painted "Jay-Z Blue." Then he starts to say something else, but stops short, explaining that he can't tell me exactly what happened to this vehicle. "That's really a Marques McCammon question," he says. "I haven't spoken to Marques in a long time."

Serch sighs.

"That Jay-Z vehicle, I never raised my voice to more people in my life," he says. "I lost my mind, and I severed ties, all my ties, with the automobile business."[1]

Jay-Z's ability to make money by attaching his name to products is one of his greatest strengths as a businessman, and it's especially important given the ever-declining numbers in the record industry. Jay-Z grossed $63 million in the twelve months before this book went to press,[2] and only about one-fifth of that came from album sales. Over the past few years, Jay-Z has shilled for Reebok, Hewlett-Packard, and Budweiser, to name a few. In the wake of my chat with Serch, it was clear that Jeep and its corporate parent, Chrysler, were slated to join that list until something went wrong.

Finding out what happened to the Jay-Z Jeep starts with Jay-Z Blue, an actual color dreamed up by Jay-Z and Steve Stoute, hip-hop's premier marketing man. Stoute began to replace Damon Dash as Jay-Z's primary business partner in 2001, after convincing Jay-Z to drop a line about Motorola in one of his songs. (The company did not return multiple phone and e-mail messages asking if Jay-Z was compensated for his services.)[3]

Regardless of whether Motorola paid Jay-Z, the shout-out signaled an awareness of the value of Jay-Z's brand and served as an early example of the many business collaborations between Stoute and the rapper. "We're pretty much joined at the hip," said Jay-Z of Stoute in 2005.[4] That same year, Stoute approached industrial designer Adrian Van Anz with the idea of creating a special shade of blue to trademark as Jay-Z's own. Van Anz, creator of the vodka-cooled computer and jewel-encrusted iPod, happily obliged by creating a reflective, silvery medium-blue color called Jay-Z Blue.[5]

The unusual blend even contained a dash of platinum dust. "Gave it a little bit of my personality," Jay-Z joked. "I'm known for platinum."[6]

Meanwhile, Stoute was elated. "We invented a color!" he gushed to the *New York Times*. "There are no limits. There is no such thing as too far."[7] Resonant with Jay-Z's *Blueprint* album and its sequels, the color could be splashed onto just about any product to create a Jay-Z edition. "Jay-Z Blue is a license for corporations to get Jay-Z in the building," Stoute explained in 2005. "Cars, laptops, lots of different things. I got deals lined up like you don't understand."[8]

The car in question was likely the sport-utility vehicle that never saw the light of day. But after a few calls to the usual industry sources, it seemed that Serch was the only person willing to even mention the Jay-Z Jeep. Steve Stoute's office never returned my messages; same for calls to Marques McCammon, who'd left Detroit for Aptera Motors, maker of bird-shaped plug-in electric vehicles. It was becoming clear that those who knew what happened to Jay-Z's eponymous automobile were not interested in sharing the story. One last hope remained: old-fashioned journalistic persistence.

Two months after my initial conversation with Serch, I find myself in a rental car on a freeway somewhere between Los Angeles and San Diego, on my way to pay a surprise visit to Marques McCammon. It occurs to me that dropping by unannounced to interview someone who may well be ignoring my calls isn't the wisest idea. Worse, I haven't developed a plan to thwart a security guard, or even a prickly receptionist. But Serch's words—"That's really a Marques McCammon question"—still echo in my head.

Upon arrival, the picture gets a bit rosier. Aptera Motors, it turns out, is housed in the first floor of an unassuming office park. The front door is locked, but a bearded man in jeans and a sweater lets me in and leads me to the front desk.

"I'm here to see Marques McCammon," I say brightly.

"Oh, he'll be back any minute," the receptionist responds.

"Great."

"Is he expecting you?"

"Well, no."

The receptionist pauses, raising her eyebrows slightly. I've blown it.

"No problem," she blurts. "Can I get you a glass of water?"

She leads me to a small conference room filled with chairs and tables that look like they're from IKEA. Five minutes later, a stocky black man who seems to be in his late thirties ambles in and introduces himself. It's Marques McCammon.

I explain that I'm writing a book on Jay-Z and that Serch said Marques was the man to talk to about the elusive Jay-Z Jeep. Much to my surprise, he nods and starts talking.

"The skinny," he says, "is this."

He lowers himself into a seat across the table from me.

"I was in the process of having some discussions with Jeep

about how they were trying to recommission their brand. They were trying to skew a little bit younger, they were getting ready to launch the Jeep Commander, the first seven-passenger Jeep to hit their portfolio. It was supposed to be the granddaddy of the Jeeps, the most luxurious."[9]

The first conversations with Jeep and parent Chrysler took place in late 2004, around the time Jay-Z was preparing to ascend to the presidency of Def Jam. The initial negotiations were part of McCammon's job at American Specialty Cars, a company often hired by Detroit automakers to make quirky-looking models like the throwback pickup Chevy SSR. Hoping to secure a contract from Chrysler to produce a souped-up version of the Jeep Commander, McCammon asked the well-connected Serch what it would take to get Jay-Z to lend his name to a special-edition Jeep Commander. "Serch was like, 'Yeah, it's gotta be the top of the line, it has to be the best of the best,'" McCammon recalls. "And that's the way Jeep was selling this truck."

So McCammon took the idea back to the executives at Mopar (short for "Motor Parts"), the automobile parts and services arm of Chrysler. With their blessing, he would have Serch reach out to Jay-Z and start the process of agreeing on terms and picking specs for the vehicle. But getting approval from the Chrysler brass proved to be a little tougher than McCammon had anticipated. "I probably went to four different executive level meetings with directors and VPs inside of marketing at Chrysler explaining [the Jay-Z Jeep concept] to them," he says. "First, one guy was like, 'Oh, Jay-Z, that's cool, but we don't want to do anything with that Puffy guy, didn't Puffy get arrested? We don't deal with anybody who got arrested.' Then somebody else found out that Jay-Z used to be a drug dealer. 'Oh, we can't do anything with that.' And I spent most of the time just trying to break down the stereotypes or the misconceptions of Jay's evolution as a person."

McCammon persisted, arguing that a Jay-Z edition Commander would be the best way to rejuvenate the brand's image. After all, Jeep had once enjoyed tremendous credibility as an urban brand in the mid-to-late 1980s. In the 1989 hit "Big Ole Butt," rapper LL Cool J dropped a reference to his "homeboy's Jeep,"[10] and he wasn't the only artist to associate himself with the brand. "Look at New Jack City, when that blew up, they bought themselves a Wrangler and ran it through Harlem," says McCammon. "Back in the day, Jeeps were the thing, but they kind of lost their flair after a while. So we thought we had a chance to bring it back."

Jay-Z seemed to be a perfect candidate to aid that effort. Fresh off the multiplatinum *Black Album* and a much-ballyhooed retirement party at Madison Square Garden, he was riding a wave of popularity that was high even by his own lofty standards. By the beginning of 2005, McCammon had prevailed upon Chrysler's executives to move forward with the Jay-Z project. Serch convinced Jay-Z's camp to get on board, and he and McCammon started brainstorming the vehicle's specs: butter-cream leather seats, twenty-two-inch chrome wheels, and a digital entertainment system preloaded with all of Jay-Z's songs. The color? Jay-Z Blue. "It was real sweet, but it wasn't gaudy," McCammon remembers. "It was really classy, kind of like the way we thought Jay would want to rep his brand."

The Jay-Z Jeep was also going to represent the interests of the rapper's bank account. According to McCammon, negotiations for his up-front fee were to start at $1 million, plus up to 5 percent of every Jay-Z Jeep sold. With its impressive list of specs, the vehicle would have retailed for about $50,000, in the neighborhood of what a normal Jeep Commander would cost with all options included. The initial run of one thousand vehicles was projected to earn Jay-Z a royalty rate of $2,500 per vehicle, or $2,500,000 in total—and exponentially more if it enjoyed the mainstream success that McCammon and Serch expected—all for simply lending his name to what was, quite literally, a cross-promotional vehicle. Says Serch: "It would have been a home run."[11]

The week before Jay-Z was set to fly to Detroit to seal the deal, McCammon called Chrysler to confirm. But in the days after McCammon convinced the company's executives of Jay-Z's legitimacy, there had been a reshuffling of management. The new boss at Mopar, the Chrysler division responsible for the deal, didn't want anything to do with Jay-Z, despite appeals from McCammon.

"I'm like, 'Dude, I've got Jay-Z flying into town,'" McCammon recounts. "'It took us a month to get on his schedule.' And I don't know if he didn't believe that we'd delivered Jay, but we kind of got brushed off. We found out later that they shifted the whole organization around, and the first guy we were talking to got moved over and moved out, and this other guy came into play. We ended up having to call Jay and renege on the meeting. Serch, of course, blew a gasket, and I came off looking like a schmuck."

McCammon and Serch have slightly different opinions on why the deal fell apart, but both agree that one of the root causes was the reluctance of Chrysler's brass—particularly, the new leadership of its Mopar division—to embrace an artist who happened to be a former drug dealer. Even in early 2005, as Jay-Z was ascending to the presidency of Def Jam, Detroit's focus wasn't on his present and future, but on his checkered past. "A lot of big corporations don't understand popular culture," says McCammon. "And they don't understand, necessarily, the story of a guy who works his way up from the street to become a prominent business person. They hear the street piece, and they get stuck on that. So I think it was a combination of the two things that really broke it down."

Serch, who is white, puts it less diplomatically. "The automobile business is run by elitist white men who are very scared of losing their power, who would rather see the whole thing crumble and fall apart than to give up their power," says Serch. "The white elitist arrogance in the automobile business is pretty much the main reason why the business has fallen apart . . . I'll stand behind that until the day I die."[12]

While McCammon pondered and Serch seethed, Jay-Z went back to business as usual. If he was upset about the downfall of his namesake Jeep, or if he shared Serch's anger toward the Detroit establishment, he didn't make a lot of noise about it. At any rate, there were plenty of other corporate suitors lining up for his endorsement services, and a few of his own deals to be made.

In 2006, the year after the Chrysler debacle, Jay-Z scored a deal to shill Hewlett-Packard. The pact included a sixty-second spot where he shows off all the things he can do with an HP Pavilion notebook. Decked in a navy suit complete with Windsor-knotted tie, he ticks through his projects, including the latest campaign for his clothing line Rocawear, plans for his upcoming world tour, and just for good measure, an online chess game. Jay-Z's association with Hewlett-Packard—and, in 2006, Armand de Brignac champagne—proved he didn't need an ailing automaker to boost his fortunes. Those deals also underscored Chrysler's myopia: Jay-Z's drug-dealing past was enough to scare a major car company into abandoning a project, yet purveyors of pricey consumer electronics and gilded bottles of French champagne were elated to receive his support. (In what was perhaps a conciliatory gesture to the hip-hop world, Chrysler featured Snoop Dogg in a series of commercials with former CEO Lee Iacocca in late 2005.[13])

Jay-Z also had deals brewing beyond the endorsement market. In the autumn of 2005, Jay-Z and two Rocawear partners paid $22 million to buy former partner Damon Dash's share of the clothing line they cofounded.[14] Barely a year later, Jay-Z and his partners made good on their investment by selling the brand to licensor Iconix for $204 million, with the potential to earn up to $35 million if the clothing line met certain sales goals.[15] As a licensor, Iconix's business plan was to scoop up valuable smaller brands and produce their goods at a lower cost than the original owners could. "They purchase the trademarks of a particular brand, which is typically the most valuable asset of a clothing company," explains Greg Weisman, a fashion industry lawyer at the firm Silver & Friedman in Los Angeles. "They believe that through their licensee network, they will be able to sell a variety of products and take it through their distribution network, which is usually wider and deeper, especially internationally, than what the original company was doing."[16]

With all the exposure it had gained through frequent mentions in Jay-Z's songs, Rocawear was a perfect acquisition target. What made this deal unique for Iconix was the level to which the former co-owner, Jay-Z, remained involved. As part of its purchase, Iconix entered into an agreement to have Jay-Z endorse, promote, and manage Rocawear and to establish a new joint venture to identify and buy new brands.[17] So even though Jay-Z was selling his equity stake, he assured himself a steady revenue stream from the company he'd just technically sold. Though Jay-Z's annual take for staying on at Rocawear wasn't specified in the SEC documents that accompanied the sale, industry sources say he receives $5 million per year for his efforts.

Trading an ownership stake for a more traditional endorsement structure plus some stock options turned out to be quite shrewd. The Iconix deal closed in March of 2007, toward the peak of the market. Did Jay-Z flip Rocawear near its highest value, on a hunch that there may have never been a better time to sell? "It sure sounds like it," says Weisman. "Most apparel [mergers and acquisitions] deals halted in somewhere between late 2008 and the beginning of 2010. . . . If you weren't set up well to absorb a 20 to 40 percent dip in your sales, you were out of business by the end of 2009."

Even with all his other business interests clicking, Jay-Z didn't forget about the auto industry. In January of 2007, just two years after the collapse of the Jay-Z Jeep deal, General Motors hosted a gaudy gala on the eve of the North American International Auto Show in a gigantic tent on the shores of the Detroit River. A procession of celebrities, including Carmen Electra and Christian Slater, escorted new vehicles down a brightly lit runway. But the star of the show was the man who emerged from a GMC Yukon—none other than Jay-Z.

The vehicle, glazed in a resplendent coat of Jay-Z Blue paint, was billed as the product of a partnership between the rapper and General Motors. Reporters on the scene were told that Jay-Z had been working closely with the company to develop the concept over the past two years. "Hopefully I'll be able to drive one of them out of here tonight," Jay-Z quipped.[18]

McCammon and Serch were livid when they heard what happened at the show. "It was the exact same thing that we'd worked up," McCammon recalls. "Jay-Z Blue, twenty-two-inch chromies. They rolled it out, and Serch sent me this note like, 'What the fuck, this is absolute bullshit.' He was completely blown."[19] To be fair, Jay-Z had every right to attach his name to any vehicle he wanted, especially since the Jay-Z Jeep fell through by no fault of his own. What frustrated Serch the most was the nature of the GM deal—though the vehicle was presented as a concept car that might hit showrooms within a couple of years, GM never had any intention of making a Jay-Z edition Yukon. "He got a really large check for coming out of that vehicle, but there was no other plan besides that," says Serch. "They didn't even show it at the auto show. That was literally just for posturing and just for the big walkout."

GM wanted Jay-Z to hop out of the Yukon for two reasons: to promote Jay-Z Blue as an option on other cars and to give their brand credibility with the millions of people who respected Jay-Z. Unlike Chrysler in 2005, GM in 2007 recognized Jay-Z's value as a marketer, past exploits and all. "The head guy at GM, he got it," says McCammon. What he didn't get, according to Serch, was that nobody would go out and buy a car based on its color. "[GM believed] that they were going to get clamors of people, of African American buyers, to go into automobile stores and ask for Jay-Z Blue— 'Can I get this vehicle in Jay-Z Blue?'—but that's not how an automobile buyer buys a vehicle," says Serch. "You have to see it. Has to be a tangible. Any real automobile guy knows this. They set it up for failure."

Sure enough, GM never produced a street-ready line of Jay-Z Yukons, and by 2008, the Jay-Z Blue idea had gone the way of Armadale Vodka. (At press time, the U.S. Patent and Trademark Office still listed "Jay-Z Blue" as a live trademark, but it often takes at least three years after a brand's demise before the department declares it dead.)[20]

Even so, that doesn't mean Jay-Z's dealings with Detroit were a failure. Yes, Chrysler backed out of the Jeep deal—thereby killing the Jay-Z Jeep—and GM never intended to see the special-edition Yukon hit the showroom floors. But in the end, Jay-Z was paid a heap of money to walk out of an SUV (Serch says the rumor in the industry was that he received a seven-figure fee).[21] Perhaps by that point, he and Steve Stoute had decided there wasn't a future for Jay-Z Blue anyway, and the Yukon deal was the best they could get. As Warren Buffett says, "Should you find yourself in a chronically leaking boat, energy devoted to changing vessels is likely to be more productive than energy devoted to patching leaks."[22] Jay-Z was wise not to spend too much time on the latter.

"The idea was great, it had great PR and buzz, I just don't know how many people were going to pay him to use his color," says media buyer Ryan Schinman. "It kind of disappeared, and nobody makes a big deal about it, but that's because it's Jay-Z and he's a risk-taker. I think everybody realizes he has this ability to try things and push the business model and change it."[23]

≡

Then again, there may yet be life in Jay-Z's seemingly moribund vehicle. In early 2010, the paparazzi spotted him in New York picking up buddy Kanye West in a silver four-door Jeep Wrangler, instead of the customary backseat of a chauffeured Maybach.[24] The appearance came just months after the release of his album *The Blueprint 3*, which features a song called "On to the Next One" and includes the line, "Bought the Jeep, tore the motherfuckin' doors off."[25]

Is the reference a meaningless lyrical detail? Is it a veiled metaphor for the failed Chrysler deal? Or is it a signal that another Jay-Z Jeep deal is in the offing? The song offers no further clues, just a warning: "Y'all should be afraid of what I'm gonna do next."

11

Reinventing the Roc

O n an empty Formula 1 race track in the shadow of a medieval castle two hours west of Frankfurt, nearly one hundred thousand people have gathered for the twenty-sixth annual edition of the German music festival Rock am Ring. The evening's roster includes guitar legend Slash and Marxist rock group Rage Against the Machine, standard fare for the rock-heavy lineup. As the sun dips behind the rolling hills to the right of the bandstand, however, a different sort of act is preparing to take the stage.

The single drum set used by the last group has been replaced with a battery of snares and cymbals, and a small platoon of guitar and brass players has coalesced in front of them. Three parallel red lines appear on the giant television screens above the stage as the speakers crackle into operation. The lights flash urgently, and the rowdy crowd slows to a murmur.

"Uh uh, uh uh," whispers a voice from offstage. "The dynasty continues."

Moments later Jay-Z saunters to the stage, clad in black jeans and a black T-shirt, with black sunglasses to match. When the band bangs out the first chords of the hit song "Run This Town," the crowd roars its approval. Then the disembodied voice of R&B star Rihanna asks who's going to run this town tonight, as if there's any doubt about Jay-Z's opinion on the matter. "We are!" he roars. "Yeah, I said it, we are / This is Roc Nation, pledge your allegiance."

By this point at a concert in any U.S. arena, nearly every member of the crowd would be putting their thumbs and fore-fingers together in a diamond shape to form the "Roc" sign, first popularized as a way of pledging allegiance to Jay-Z's original Roc-A-Fella Records. In Europe, where Jay-Z is a relative unknown compared to his wife, Beyoncé, inspiring blind devotion takes a bit more work.

"Everybody put your diamonds in the air," he instructs the audience as he begins his third song, demonstrating with his own hands. Sure enough, a sea of arms rises to form Jay-Z's logo. The exercise complete, he launches into a series of his most bombastic ballads, starting with the stomping beat of "On to the Next One." Less than halfway through the show, Jay-Z seems to have won over the last holdouts in the writhing mass of humanity before him. Toward the end of his set, he launches into his international hit "Big Pimpin'" but deliberately stops the song a few measures in. When the crowd moans in distress, he tells them he won't start up again until everybody grabs something to wave around in the air. Within seconds, a vast swarm of makeshift cheerleading equipment swirls into the twilight—sweaters, scarves, flags, even an inflatable cow—and Jay-Z restarts his song to thunderous applause.

In a balcony high above, reserved for press and VIPs, a bespectacled man in a suit turns to me and smiles, motioning toward the crumbling fortress in the distance.

"Imagine," he shouts above the din in a heavy German accent, "what the guy would think who built that castle!"

The jubilant scene in Germany was part of Jay-Z's Blueprint 3 tour, a sixty-two-show international extravaganza that ended in 2010. The tour likely wouldn't have been possible— or at least, it wouldn't have been quite as profitable—were it not for a career-defining megadeal whose cogs were set in motion years earlier.

In December of 2007, Jay-Z was growing restless as his three-year contract to preside over Def Jam approached expiration. After launching the solo careers of stars like Rihanna, Kanye West, and Ne-Yo, he felt he'd proven himself as a record label executive. His own musical career was once again on the rise, and he'd handled the bootlegging of his latest album with grace; *American Gangster* went on to become his tenth platinum solo effort.

Def Jam's situation wasn't looking quite as rosy, but that was more a reflection of a music business trend than Jay-Z's management skills—industry-wide album sales fell from eight hundred million in 2000 to four hundred million in 2008.[1] Jay-Z figured he was worth more than the roughly $10 million annual salary he'd been earning as president. "I felt underutilized," he later explained. "To me it was like, 'I've sold companies for huge amounts of money. I'm an entrepreneur— that's what I've been all my life. I can't just sit here and make records and not do anything else.' "[2] He tried to convince Def Jam to bring him back in an unorthodox new role in which he'd help the label make money in the industry's shifting landscape. "I told them, 'How about this idea—instead of spending $300 million to break four acts, why don't you guys give me a credit line, and I'll just go do things. I won't make music. I'll go buy some headphones, or buy a clothing line, just be part of the culture.' But the money scared them off, because they're not used to thinking that way."[3]

On Christmas Eve of 2007, Jay-Z announced that he wouldn't be returning to his post at Def Jam for a fourth year. "I am pleased to have had the opportunity to build upon the Def Jam legacy," he said in a written statement. "Now it's time for me to take on new challenges." If Jay-Z left because Def Jam wasn't willing to give him the new authority he desired, his former bosses gave no indication. "While [Jay-Z] will continue to be one of our signature artists, he will nonetheless be missed in this executive capacity," declared Antonio "L.A." Reid, the chairman of Island Def Jam.[4]

From Jay-Z's perspective, the appeal of forging ahead on his own outweighed the draw of Def Jam's traditional label structure. "It's really about trying to invest in the future, trying to invest in maybe coming up with a new model," he said shortly after his exit. "Because going in hard making records with artists and throwing those records into a system that's flawed is not exciting for me . . . My whole thing is, how do we invest in the future? If everyone is committed to doing that, then I'm sure there's a deal to be made."[5]

The blogosphere buzzed with all sorts of interesting possibilities as to what his next move would be. At various points, speculation swirled of an impending collaboration with Apple or a super-label with Beyoncé, or both. But once Jay-Z moved on from Def Jam, the first months of 2008 passed without any of the rumors coming to fruition. Between launching 40/40 Club locations in Atlantic City and Las Vegas (the latter has since closed), becoming more active as a shareholder in the Nets, and brainstorming ideas for the final album he owed Def Jam under his artist agreement, Jay-Z had plenty of work to keep himself occupied. It seemed he wasn't planning to conquer any new frontiers anytime soon.

In April of 2008, however, the proverbial other S. Carter sneaker finally dropped. Jay-Z and concert promoter Live Nation announced that they were joining forces as part of a ten-year, $150-million agreement. The pact consolidated all of Jay-Z's music-related ventures—touring, recording, and management of other artists—under the Live Nation umbrella. Because his new deal encompassed recorded music,

Jay-Z had to pay Def Jam $5 million to buy out his contractual obligation to make one final album. "I wanted to have it back for a number of reasons, the most important being that it wasn't consistent with the type of business I planned," he explained. "It was moreso the principle than the amount of money. It was about owning my own masters and owning my own companies, but you have to pay for the privilege."[6]

Principle aside, the $5 million buyout was an excellent business move—and likely a greater motivation than the notion of gaining full control of his masters, which were set to revert to him in 2012 anyway under his expiring Def Jam deal. In the new agreement, Live Nation paid Jay-Z an advance of $10 million for the bought-out album that would become *The Blueprint 3* and promised him the same amount for at least three albums over the course of the ten-year deal. The rest of the pact encompassed many slices of his business, making it one of the most prominent examples of a so-called 360-degree deal: he received an upfront payment of $25 million plus an additional $20 million for certain publishing and licensing rights. (He kept his masters, though one lawyer familiar with the matter points out that there was a "fairly complicated and strenuous licensing agreement which some people might consider equivalent to a sale [of his masters]."[7]) He also received $50 million to cover costs of starting a new record label and talent agency called Roc Nation, as well as a general touring advance of $25 million. "I've turned into the Rolling Stones of hip-hop," Jay-Z told the *New York Times* shortly after signing.[8]

Jay-Z's proclamation wasn't far from the truth. The touring portion of his pact gave him the big-budget backing he needed to elevate his live performances to a new level, both in terms of production value and financial success. On 1999's Hard Knock Life tour, widely considered the most successful hip-hop tour of its day, Jay-Z had to split each concert's ticket sales of $375,000 with coheadliner DMX and a host of lesser rappers. After paying sound engineers, stage technicians, and the like, even the best artists only take home a third of their gross ticket sales, so Jay-Z's gain was likely in the neighborhood of $60,000 per show, meaning he netted less than $3 million on the forty-eight-show tour—before taxes.[9]

The Rolling Stones, on the other hand, grossed $558 million from 2005 to 2007 on a 144-show tour, the most remunerative in history.[10] Even after whittling down the group's take to account for expenses using the same one-third formula, each of the four Stones walked away with about $325,000 per show before taxes, or nearly $50 million per member over the course of the tour. Considering that breakdown, it's not hard to see why Jay-Z would want to be the Rolling Stones of hip-hop.

The disparity in earnings between the two acts can be traced to a simple equation: convince fifty thousand people to pay an average of $80 per seat every night, and you, too, can be the Rolling Stones. Getting that many fans to pay that much to see a concert is something that only a few acts, usually limited to mainstream rock groups, can achieve. According to Nielsen SoundScan, rock is the most popular genre of music, selling 124 million records in 2009. That's far more than alternative (68 million), country (46 million), and rap (26 million),[11] and those numbers translate to huge crowds when acts like the Rolling Stones, U2, Bruce Springsteen, and the Eagles go on tour.

The paradigm for hip-hop concerts is totally different. Because the genre's audience is roughly one-fourth the size of rock's following, it's nearly impossible for even the most prominent hip-hop acts to pack an eighty-thousand-seat football stadium; twenty-thousand-seat basketball and hockey arenas are basically the limit. And unlike rock, which typically features a live band with a singer and at least three instrumentalists, rap concerts center on a DJ at a turntable and an MC rapping over the beats, leaving fewer elements that can be varied in a live show. A skilled turntablist can please the crowd with tricks like "scratching"—moving vinyl records back and forth with one's fingers, thereby producing the sort of electronic ripping noise popularized by early hip-hop music—and by seamlessly segueing from one song to another. But if the DJ isn't creative, rap concerts can sometimes sound like the MC is simply rapping over recorded music.

There have long been other, more insidious factors working against the viability of hip-hop tours. Until Jay-Z's Hard Knock Life excursion changed the landscape in the late 1990s, prevailing attitudes made it nearly impossible to conduct a large-scale hip-hop tour at all. "Concert promoters and the venues were driving prices so high for rap concerts

REINVENTING THE ROC **193**

and security, by the time you finished paying for all of that you couldn't put out a decent rap show. . . . But we showed that it could be done," Jay-Z explained in 2005. "Once I got to a certain point in my career, I realized the things I did affected hip-hop and black people as a whole."[12]

One of the things Jay-Z did was to blaze a trail for hip-hop acts at rock music festivals. Shortly after signing his deal with Live Nation in 2008, he headlined the Glastonbury Festival in the United Kingdom. Many spoke out against bringing in a rapper to play a traditionally rock-focused show, including Noel Gallagher of the rock group Oasis, who said that Glastonbury's organizers had made the wrong decision. Critics predicted Jay-Z would be booed off the stage. But when Jay-Z took the stage weeks later and opened his set with a bold parody of the Oasis song "Wonderwall," he immediately won the crowd. "Both audience and artist rose to the occasion and turned in a moment of real, euphoric, pop-culture history," declared the *Sunday Times*. "His performance will go down in Glastonbury history," chimed the *Independent*.[13]

As his career progressed, Jay-Z began to see a spike in his touring earnings. He cleared roughly $60,000 on revenues of about $200,000 per show in 1999; by 2003, his take-home fee jumped from $100,000 to $300,000 per show while on tour with 50 Cent.[14] When he signed with Live Nation five years later, Jay-Z eliminated the need to rely on a coheadliner to help bankroll the shows. These days, Jay-Z is more Springsteen than Snoop Dogg. Under his Live Nation deal, each show is a near carbon copy of the musical spectacle described at the beginning of this chapter. There's a big-budget rocker-style entrance, the full brass band, and the dual drum sets. Instrumental music from a living, breathing backup band is something few mainstream hip-hop acts can boast. As a result, Jay-Z's average gross per concert since signing with Live Nation is over $1 million—nearly twice as much as Lil Wayne, the next most successful live rapper.[15]

While working as Def Jam's president, Jay-Z essentially went on a three-year hiatus from touring. He returned with his sixty-two-show Blueprint 3 tour, which started in the fall of 2009 and grossed roughly $60 million in ticket sales, to say nothing of merchandise. If the eight hundred thousand people who attended Jay-Z's latest tour each spent an average of $10 on merchandise (T-shirts, posters, etc.), that's an additional $8 million to split between Jay-Z and Live Nation. All in all, that means Jay-Z's net earnings for less than a year of touring were about $25 million, roughly three times his annual salary as a Def Jam executive.

"Jay can look at Live Nation as his music unit, I suppose," says Jeff Chang. "If you've got so much other business going on, you want a unit taking care of that part of your career."[16] As such, Live Nation took over the tasks previously reserved for record labels: producing and promoting records. In the past, labels would give an artist an advance for an album, and tours would be handled separately by a concert promoter. In Jay-Z's deal, the concert promoter received a slice of all his music-related revenue streams—touring, merchandizing, record sales, etc.—in exchange for a hefty upfront fee and profit split.

Jay-Z's 360-degree deal was the latest evolution of a type of agreement whose roots date back to the 1960s. In those days, a few groups like the Partridge Family and the Monkees were signed to "multiple rights" deals. These acts were conceived entirely by music industry executives, and group members were simply hired as employees. Record labels owned the rights to everything associated with the bands, including their names. In 2007, British pop star Robbie Williams became the first independent act to sign a 360-degree deal, inking an 80-million-pound pact (about $120 million at the 2002 exchange rate) with EMI. Madonna followed by signing a ten-year, $150-million deal with Live Nation in 2007, paving the way for Jay-Z's deal in 2008.[17]

The motivation for record companies to sign acts to 360-degree deals isn't hard to understand. In 2008, ticket prices for the top one hundred tours averaged $67, more than double the 1998 average; album sales plummeted. In 2007, the Institute for Policy Innovation reported that U.S. recording firms were losing $5 billion per year to music piracy.[18] The 360-degree template represented a chance for labels to get a cut of something that couldn't be copied and shared over the Internet: revenues from ticket and merchandise sales.

For the upstart Live Nation, 360-degree deals were a way to lure artists from the traditional record labels that were trying to get in on the lucrative touring business. Flush with cash from its late-2005 initial public offering on the New York Stock Exchange, Live Nation threw gobs of money at big acts like Jay-Z and Madonna, partly in the form of stock options. Jay-Z's deal included 775,000 shares of Live Nation, along with an option to purchase 500,000 more—bringing his equity stake to nearly 1 percent of the company (at the time this book went to press, his shares were worth about $12 million). Shakira and Nickelback, two other acts signed by Live Nation, did not receive stock options. For savvier artists like Jay-Z and Madonna, the negotiations were a bonanza.[19]

"Live Nation did these huge deals largely on the terms of the artist," explains Dina LaPolt, an entertainment lawyer who specializes in multiple-rights deals. "Normally, the record company has a lot of leverage, and the artist is really very limited in what rights they can kick out and what rights they have to be stuck giving the record company. But in the case of the 360-degree deals with Live Nation and Jay-Z and Madonna and all them, those artists had significant amounts of leverage and significant bargaining power because they were so successful. . . . They were able to extract millions and millions of dollars from Live Nation."[20]

Just as he did with Iconix, Jay-Z seemed to sense both the desperation of his corporate quarry and the proximity of the market's peak. His $150-million pact was, along with Madonna's, the largest handed out by Live Nation. By the time the world economy went into a tailspin six months later, Jay-Z had guaranteed himself an annual eight-figure salary for the coming decade, and Live Nation had stopped handing out massive multiple-rights deals to musical acts.

"Those deals aren't happening anymore," says LaPolt. "Jay-Z is an astute business person, and all of his advisers are really, really impeccable. So if they did the deal, it's because it was good for Jay-Z. That's the one thing we do as practitioners— when someone's giving us money, our job is to structure the rights [so that] we give as limited an amount of rights for the most money we possibly can get. That deal was something that was turned over, upside down, left, right, and center by his representatives."

Though the timing of Jay-Z's deal was uncanny and its scope staggering, perhaps the most unusual part was the musical joint venture it created. Live Nation's executives recognized that Jay-Z, far more than any of the other recording artists it had signed, had both a thirst and an aptitude for entrepreneurship. They also recognized that he was serious in his demands that an outlet for such desires be a part of any deal he signed. Under these auspices, Roc Nation was born. "The Jay-Z deal was unique in that it came with a caveat that he was able to develop this company with Live Nation," says LaPolt. "He was actually [going to be] signing and managing and developing new talent."

Using a clever moniker to evoke both Live Nation's name and Jay-Z's Roc-A-Fella Records roots, Roc Nation was founded as just the sort of next-generation musical venture that Jay-Z had envisioned as he was leaving Def Jam. The company was set up as a miniature entertainment conglomerate, complete with arms for creative consulting, publishing, and management for artists, songwriters, producers, and sound engineers. Roc Nation was also a record label, but not in the traditional sense of the term. Rather than build up an expensive production infrastructure, its model was to distribute albums in one-off deals with existing record labels (Jay-Z's *Blueprint 3* was distributed by Atlantic Records). All of Roc Nation's artists would be signed to 360-degree deals, albeit at a much lower rate than the one their boss scored.

For the up-and-coming acts themselves, multiple-rights deals have always been somewhat dangerous. Since most young artists tend not to have a great deal of leverage in their negotiations, they traditionally sign fairly cheap deals with record companies in the hopes of getting famous in time to score a more lucrative second contract. In the meantime, they can always make money by touring. Under a 360-degree deal, they're locked into that low-paying deal across all of their revenue streams.

"I think the 360-degree deals make a lot of sense if you're an established legacy artist," says entertainment lawyer Bernie Resnick. "But they're very dangerous for emerging acts because all of your eggs are now in one basket."[21]

Still, there aren't many aspiring musicians who would turn down a record deal. And unsurprisingly, Jay-Z didn't have much trouble finding artists to populate Roc Nation's lineup. In February 2009, he signed rapper Jermaine Cole, better known by his stage name, J. Cole, to be Roc Nation's inaugural artist. A communications major at St. John's University before joining Roc Nation, Cole was well aware of his role. "If it wasn't for [Jay-Z], they wouldn't even be talking about me," he told *XXL* months after signing. "So until I put out an album, make a classic, put out hit singles, I'm gonna be Jay-Z's artist. But the only thing that's gonna get me out of his shadow is building my own shadow."[22]

As he showed during his tenure at Def Jam, Jay-Z has a knack for scouting and developing undiscovered talent. Somewhere along the way, he picked up the ability to make young artists and ordinary people feel at ease around him, a skill that came in handy in his new role as head of Roc Nation. Nick Simmons, an aspiring music executive, witnessed this quality firsthand while working as a Def Jam intern under Jay-Z. By 2009, Simmons had worked his way into a full-time job at Columbia Records, the Sony-backed label contracted to distribute J. Cole's first album. As soon as that deal was finalized, Jay-Z scheduled a meeting between his team at Roc Nation and the folks at Columbia. Simmons remembers the reaction in the conference room that day.

"All of a sudden, the door opens, and Jay-Z walks in, and everybody just claps—standing ovation," he recalls. "So then we go around, and everybody introduces themselves at the table, and it's still kind of tense. People are stuttering, like 'I—I—I'm this person, and I do this.' Jay-Z is the last person to introduce himself, and he just says, 'Jiggaman, ya heard?' Everybody started laughing and that just eased the whole tension and the mood in the room. So, I believe he knows he has a presence around people, and I guess that was his way to break the ice with us, to make us feel comfortable around him."²³

What impressed Simmons even more than Jay-Z's ability to lighten the boardroom mood was his command of the situation at hand. "He essentially told us the meeting was all about business, and, from my experience, that's what he's about—business," Simmons recalls. "He told us what he wanted, what he expected from J. Cole, what he wanted the plan to be. He said, 'J. Cole's young, he's a college graduate, he should hit these markets, the college market, we're going on a college tour.'"

Then Jay-Z asked who was in charge of college marketing. "The guy raised his hand, and Jay-Z said, 'I need to talk to you 'cause this is a big initiative,'" Simmons recounts. "So he just sat at the meeting, and he told everybody, 'This is what we need to do: radio people need to target this song, we're going to go with this song, we should have a single out by here. We don't want to rush this project, we want to have grassroots marketing.' He had a plan, and he just laid it out for everybody."

There were other impressive aspects to Jay-Z's marketing plan for J. Cole. When Jay-Z was putting together his own first album for Roc Nation, he prominently featured J. Cole on a track called "A Star Is Born." When *XXL* magazine put Jay-Z on its cover in October 2009, the issue also featured a story on J. Cole (not to mention a twenty-four-page spread of

Rocawear ads at the front of the book and over twenty pages of editorial content focused on Jay-Z). Knowing Jay-Z's tendencies, none of this was a coincidence.

"Powerful artists often negotiate with editors for package deals," says music professor and journalist Elizabeth Mendez Berry. "So it'll be, 'Okay, I'll be on the cover, but you have to cover this artist I'm working with. You have to do this feature, that feature.' It's a way for them to use their own popularity to promote their protégés."[24]

J. Cole, then, is simply the latest beneficiary of Jay-Z's business smarts, though it's clear his boss pays him a bit of extra attention. "I can tell he's very protective because this is his first artist," says Simmons. "He wants to make sure everything goes perfectly."

Perfection is a tall order, but Jay-Z's first two years at the helm of Roc Nation have included plenty of highlights. In addition to releasing a tremendously popular album of his own and completing one of the most profitable hip-hop tours in history, Jay-Z has lured new artists including Wale, Mark Ronson, and The Ting Tings to his company's management wing. He has also spearheaded joint ventures to create cobranded memorabilia with the New York Yankees and a line of headphones with Skullcandy. He'll have to keep up that pace to make Roc Nation a long-term success. For now, though, he's already delivering on his promise to create a new kind of music company—the kind he left Def Jam to start.

12

History and Beyond

Not all of Jay-Z's ventures have gone perfectly. His entrepreneurial wastepaper basket is filled with scuttled plans for a Jay-Z Jeep, a failed Las Vegas nightclub, and an aborted casino and racetrack project in New York.[1] But most moguls have had their share of failures, and they survive on the strength of new ideas good enough to erase the bad memories. Few will remember that Steve Jobs was once fired from Apple; instead, they'll remember how he came back and revitalized the company he founded by creating the iPod.

Jay-Z's business career will be known for its highlights—Live Nation, the Nets, Rocawear—and other deals he makes in the coming years. He won't be remembered for the mentors he's cast aside, but rather for the protégés whose careers he's helped launch, including Kanye West, Rihanna, Rick Ross, Ne-Yo, and J. Cole. He has expanded his own musical tastes, popping up at performances by alternative groups like Muse and Grizzly Bear and even collaborating with rock acts like Santigold and Chris Martin. His 2010 album *The Blueprint 3* was not only one of his most eclectic, but one of his most successful in terms of pop-culture appeal. "It's a credit to Jay-Z's longevity," says Craig Kallman, chief of Atlantic Records. "The fact that he had his crowning creative achievement in terms of radio and global reach with this album is remarkable this far into his career."[2]

Meanwhile, Jay-Z's entrepreneurial impulses only seem to be growing more refined and international in scope. In 2005, he bought a large chunk of The Spotted Pig, a Michelin-spangled gastro pub in the West Village.[3] In 2009, he joined Will Smith and Jada Pinkett-Smith to invest $1 million in the Tony Award–winning Broadway show *Fela!*[4] The following year, Jay-Z suggested he might be interested in buying a stake in the English Premier League's Arsenal soccer team. "I don't know a lot about the business of soccer, but in the future if the right opportunity presented itself, then who knows?" he said. "I am a businessman, and I will always look at an opportunity."[5]

With a personal fortune of roughly half a billion dollars and a place in hip-hop's pantheon already secured, it would seem that Jay-Z has few reasons to keep working, let alone take on a challenge as difficult as buying a foreign soccer team. Yet he still makes new music and pursues uncharted business ventures with more rigor than ever. Some observers would point to his seemingly infinite desire for wealth and fame, spurred by the insecurity and poverty of his youth.

Jay-Z might say it's something a bit nobler—the perfection of his legacy. He rarely waxes sentimental, but his song "History" is about as close as he gets to all-out schmaltz. After alluding to the poignant hopes of his early life ("All I got is dreams, nobody else can see / Nobody else believes, nobody else but me"), he explains his journey to the top by likening abstract concepts to fictional women. Until he finds Victory ("She keeps eluding me"), he's stuck with Success ("She's good to the touch, she's good for the moment, but she's never enough"). Once he finally wins Victory, they'll have a child ("We'll have a baby who stutters repeatedly, we'll name him History"). The song's final verse offers a compelling glimpse into the soul behind Jay-Z's invincible exterior: "Long after I'm gone, long after I breathe / I leave all I am in the hands of History."[6]

I've been sitting with DJ Clark Kent at the Applebee's in Brooklyn for nearly three hours. The winter sun is sinking toward the snow-covered rooftops along Flatbush Avenue, and our margaritas have been reduced to puddles of ice and salt. Kent is still riffing on Jay-Z.

"I think it's unfair to call Jay-Z a rapper," he says. "I think rapping is something he *does*. When he says, 'I'm not a businessman—I'm a business, man,' you really have to take that seriously. He is a business, and rapping is just something that's in his business."[7]

Kent toys with the swizzle stick in the empty glass on the table in front of him.

"There's people who sit around saying they want to be Bill Gates, but there's way more people who say they want to be Jay-Z," he muses. "They don't know who Bill Gates is. Jay-Z's probably sitting around going, 'I want to be Bill Gates to the tenth power.'"

With that, Kent pulls out his BlackBerry. It's later than he thought—time to go. He shakes my hand and scoots out of the booth. As he's putting on his overcoat, he offers a final thought about how history will view Shawn Carter.

"He's not a rapper, he's not an entertainer," says Kent. "He's a Jay-Z."

ACKNOWLEDGMENTS

This book nearly ended before I had the chance to start it. I was at home with the flu on a sweaty summer afternoon—feverishly banishing unwanted press invitations and Nigerian bank transfer scams from my inbox—when I chanced upon an e-mail with the subject line "Book Project Opportunity with Portfolio (Penguin)." My addled brain didn't register that this might be a message worth reading until my index finger was descending upon the delete key. Many thanks to Jillian Gray, the sender of the message and the editor of this book, for reaching out to a writer even younger than Jay-Z was upon the debut of his first album. If it weren't for Jillian, Adrian Zackheim, and the rest of the folks at Penguin/Portfolio, I might have been selling my first book out of a car trunk as well. My eternal gratitude goes to my agents, Ed Victor and William Clark. I dread to think what I would have done without William's encouragement and Ed's advice ("You shouldn't begin your book proposal by saying you were searching for an anecdote for your book proposal!").

I wouldn't have been in a position to write this book without the support of my friends and mentors at *Forbes*. I will be forever grateful to Mary Ellen Egan and Stewart Pinkerton, for hiring me; to Lea Goldman, for handing me her hip-hop Rolodex; to Dan Bigman, for putting me in charge of *Forbes*'s hip-hop coverage; to Tom Post, for the honesty of his editing; and to Bruce Upbin, who is a much better editor than a fantasy sportsman. A big thank-you to Lewis D'Vorkin, Matt Schifrin, and Neil Weinberg for their good judgment and continued support. Thanks also to David Randall, Asher Hawkins, Emily Schmall, Hana Alberts, and Peter Schwartz for camaraderie and encouragement, and to Bill Baldwin, Larry Reibstein, Kurt Badenhausen, Dave Whelan, Jim Clash, and Dave Serchuk for their guidance. An extra helping of gratitude to Carrie Coolidge, Sue Radlauer, and the members of *Forbes*'s copy desk, who've saved me from untold embarrassment.

Jay-Z straddles the line between two worlds; appropriately, the bulk of this book was written from an apartment located on the dividing line between Harlem and the Upper East Side of Manhattan. Other parts of this book were conceived, written, debated, reported, and edited in a variety of states, both geographical and mental. For generous hospitality and creative support, many thanks to Susan Calhoun, Charlie Moss, Suzanne Maas, Julia Bradford, and Charlie Warner in New York; William Christian, Daniela Sloninsky, and Matt Lachman in California; Terry Fixel and Gus La Rocco in Florida; Addison, Jaden, Joslin, Maggie, and Joel Peck in Illinois; Bridget, Neil, Mary Beth, James, and Irma

O'Malley in Texas; and Sebastian Hain and Sarah Hellriegel in Germany.

A book is nothing without good sources, and that's doubly true when the book is unauthorized. Thanks to sources-turned-friends and friends-turned-sources, especially Patti Silverman, Nick Simmons, Sarah Vass, Diana Liao, Eric Arnold, Lacey Rose, Branson, Fab, Serch, and "Deep Throat" in Santa Monica; as well as those who provided a constant stream of Jay-Z news that not even my Google Alert could rival—Hannah Elliott, Janine Lebofsky, Deepak Thosar, and Jon, Naomi, and Lee Peck. Thanks to Alman Shibli for his insight into the tonal qualities of flow, to Elizabeth Mendez Berry and Touré for sharing their personal impressions of Jay-Z, and to Damien McCaffery for a very helpful last-minute read.

A big thank-you for unwavering support from old friends: Ryan Victor, Sam Moss, Luke Silver-Greenberg, Morgan Silver-Greenberg, Madeline Kerner, Kelly Reid, and Corey Taylor; slightly newer: Dan Adler, Jon Bittner, Rebecca Blum, Katie Manning, Dan Hammond, Lara Berlin, and Marcus Leonard; newest: the Mount Sinai Class of 2013. Special thanks to Melissa Ocana and Ezra Markowitz, who repeatedly called from Oregon to make sure I hadn't (completely) lost my mind, and to the artist formerly known as Nick Messitte-Greenberg for a ruthlessly thoughtful read.

Sanity is something I wouldn't have had without the comrades who joined me at trivia in Brooklyn nearly every Tuesday night during the writing of this book. Without Andrew

Cedotal, Nicole Villeneuve, Mallory Hellman, Laurie Burkitt, Mike Seplowitz, Lauren Henry, Francesca Levy, and Bethany Kerner, my life would be comparatively devoid of errata and camaraderie. My endless gratitude goes to Jon Bruner, who, despite not knowing how to pronounce the name of Jay-Z's wife, provided unwavering support of the technical, editorial, and miscellaneous variety. A big truckful of thanks to Julien Dumoulin-Smith, both for reading this book on a flight home from Dubai and for a friendship without which I wouldn't know anything about business *or* hip-hop.

Thanks to my mother, Suzanne O'Malley, who taught me a lot of things—perhaps most of all that being in the right place at the right time isn't a matter of luck, but rather a matter of putting yourself there. To my honorary mother Judith Greenburg, whose thoughtful and thorough feedback dramatically improved the quality of this book, and whose comments served as a litmus test for rap lingo ("What's the derivation of 'Hov'? Dan suggests it may refer to Jehovah, which would be very interesting . . ."). To my father, Dan Greenburg, my toughest critic and biggest fan. Dad, on both counts and for the example you set both as a writer and as a person, I can't thank you enough.

The biggest possible thank-you goes to Danielle La Rocco, my best friend, lover, muse, adviser, doctor, and editor. Thanks generally for being wonderful and specifically for putting up with my neurotic writer behavior, including late-night inspection of Jay-Z lyrics ("It sounds like you're building a railroad in there!"), the pot of cooked pasta I left on the stove overnight, and my recurring dreams of conversing with Jay-Z inside a Duane Reade.

I wish that Leah Greenburg, Sam Greenburg, Don O'Malley, Pat O'Malley, and Françoise Dumoulin could be here to read this book. I'm deeply saddened that Andrew Clancy will never get the chance to write his own.

Finally, I'd like to thank Jay-Z for living a life worth chronicling.

NOTES

Introduction

1   *New York Times* staff, "1,200 on Last Trip on Myrtle Ave.
     El," *New York Times*, October 4, 1969.

2   Jay-Z, "Moment of Clarity," *The Black Album*, Roc-A-Fella
     Records, 2003.

3   Lisa Taddeo, "Jay-Z: It Takes a Harmless, Hand-Built
     Gangster to Run This Town," *Esquire*, January 7, 2010.

4   Adam Sherwin, "Blinged Up Wellies for Glastonbury Arrive
     at Jay-Z's Hotel," *The Times* (London), June 26, 2008.

5   Dorothy Pomerantz and Lacey Rose, "The Celebrity 100,"
     Forbes, June 28, 2010, http://www.forbes.com/2010/06/22/
     lady-gaga-oprah-winfrey-business-entertainment-celeb-
     100-10_land.html.

6   Scott DeCarlo, "What the Boss Makes," *Forbes*, April 28,
     2010, http://www.forbes.com/2010/04/27/compensation-
     chief-executive-salary-leadership-boss-10-ceo-
     compensation-intro.html. Note: List tabulates CEO pay by
     combining salary and exercised stock options or vested stock
     awards.

7   Kanye West featuring Jay-Z, "Diamonds from Sierra Leone (Remix)," *Late Registration*, Def Jam/Roc-A-Fella Records, 2005.

8   Craig Kallman, electronic message to author, August 2010.

9   Russell Simmons, "Jay-Z," *Newsweek*, November 13, 2009, http://2010.newsweek.com/top-10/newly-minted-tycoons/jay-z-and-beyonce.html.

10 Shawn Carter Scholarship Fund staff, "About Us," Shawn Carter Scholarship Fund Web site, http://shawncartersf.com/AboutUs.aspx?p=about.

11 Jonathan Lemire, "Stars Guide Donors' Way," *New York Daily News*, September 2, 2005.

12 Nick Wadhams, "Jay-Z Helps U.N. Focus on Water Crisis," Associated Press, August 9, 2006.

13 Nekesa Mumbi Moody, "Organizers Say All-Star 'Hope for Haiti Now' Telethon Raises $57M for Quake Victims, So Far," Associated Press, January 23, 2010.

14 Jonathan "Jaz-O" Burks, telephone interview by author, May 2010.

15 Bonsu Thompson, "'Bout Me," *XXL*, October 2009.

16 Mark Binelli, "King of America," *Rolling Stone*, June 24, 2010.

Chapter 1: A Hard Knock Life

1   Touré, "The Book of Jay," *Rolling Stone*, December 15, 2005.

2   *NY-Z*, mini-documentary, directed by Danny Clinch, 2009, http://www.youtube.com/watch?v=Q6zVR0SgSOM.

3   Touré, "The Book of Jay," *Rolling Stone*, December 15, 2005.

4   Ibid.

5   Jay-Z, "Moment of Clarity," *The Black Album*, Roc-A-Fella
    Records, 2003.

6   Jay-Z, "December 4th," *The Black Album*, Roc-A-Fella
    Records, 2003.

7   Rodolfo "DJ Clark Kent" Franklin, interview by author,
    Brooklyn, New York, January 2010.

8   Jonathan "Jaz-O" Burks, interview by author, May 2010.

9   Touré, "The Book of Jay," *Rolling Stone*, December 15, 2005.

10 Jonathan "Jaz-O" Burks, electronic message to author, July
    2010.

11 Jay-Z, "You Must Love Me," *In My Lifetime Vol. I*, Roc-A-
    Fella Records, 1997.

12 Ibid.

13 Ibid.

14 David Kohn, "The King of Rap," *CBS News*, August 13,
    2002, http://www.cbsnews.com/stories/2002/11/18/60II/
    main529811.shtml.

15 Jay-Z, "December 4th," *The Black Album*, Roc-A-Fella
    Records, 2003.

16 Carlos R. Martinez, electronic message to author, November
    2009.

17 Billy Valdez, electronic message to author, November 2009.

18 Salvador Contes, telephone interview by author, December
    2009.

19 DeHaven Irby, interview by author, Brooklyn, New York,
    January 2010.

20 Ibid.

21 Elvis Mitchell, "Jay-Z," *Interview*, February 2010.

22 Jay-Z, "December 4th," *The Black Album*, Roc-A-Fella Records, 2003.

23 Michael "DJ Serch" Berrin, telephone interview by author, December 2009.

24 Jay-Z, "The Takeover," *The Blueprint*, Roc-A-Fella Records, 2001.

25 Larry Collins, "The Seeds of Misery—Crack," *Sunday Times*, November 14, 1993.

26 Jay-Z, "December 4th," *The Black Album*, Roc-A-Fella Records, 2003.

27 Terry Williams, *Crackhouse: Notes from the End of the Line* (New York: Penguin, 1993), p. 8.

28 Michael "MC Serch" Berrin, electronic message to author, August 2010.

29 Donald David, telephone interview by author, July 2010.

30 Patrick "A Kid Called Roots" Lawrence, interview by author, New York, November 2009.

31 Touré, telephone interview by author, December 2009.

32 Jay-Z, "Dead Presidents," *Reasonable Doubt*, Roc-A-Fella Records, 1996.

33 Richard Harrington, "Jay-Z's Rhymes of Passion," *Washington Post*, January 2, 2000.

34 Touré, "The Book of Jay," *Rolling Stone*, December 15, 2005.

35 Kanye West featuring Jay-Z, "Diamonds from Sierra Leone (Remix)," *Late Registration*, Def Jam/Roc-A-Fella Records, 2005.

Chapter 2: The Roc-A-Fella Dynasty

1 Christian Koch, "Nice Threads," *Evening Standard*, March 15, 2010.

2 Victoria Newton, "Becks Sees Stab Victim," *Sun*, July 15, 2003.

3 Damon Dash, telephone interview by author, January 2010.

4 Elizabeth Mendez Berry, interview by author, New York, New York, May 2010.

5 Donald David, telephone interview by author, July 2010.

6 Patrick "A Kid Called Roots" Lawrence, interview by author, New York, New York, November 2009.

7 Michael "MC Serch" Berrin, interview by author, December 2009.

8 Jay-Z, "Can't Knock the Hustle," *Reasonable Doubt*, Roc-A-Fella Records, 1996.

9 *XXL* Staff, "The Making of Reasonable Doubt," *XXL*, August 2006.

10 Michael "MC Serch" Berrin, interview by author, December 2009.

11 Ryan Schinman, telephone interview by author, June 2009. Note: Excerpts from this interview appeared in my article "Michael Jackson's Estate Sale," *Forbes*, June 27, 2009, http://www.forbes.com/2009/06/26/michael-jackson-beatles-business-media-estate.html.

12 Jay-Z, "No Hook," *American Gangster*, Roc-A-Fella Records, 2007.

13 Michael "MC Serch" Berrin, electronic message to author, August 2010.

14 Eric Konigsberg, "Why Damon Dash Hates Mondays," *New York* magazine, June 11, 2006.

15 Jon Caramanica, "Jay-Z," in *The New Rolling Stone Album Guide, Ed. 4*, ed. Nathan Brackett and Christian Hoard (New York: Fireside, 2004), p. 424.

16 VH1 staff, "100 Greatest Songs of the '90s," *VH1*, December 13, 2007, http://blog.vh1.com/2007-12-13/top-100-songs-of-the-90s/.

17 Recording Industry Association of America database, "Gold and Platinum (Jay-Z)," Recording Industry Association of America, http://www.riaa.com/goldandplatinumdata.php?table=SEARCH_RESULTS.

18 Jay-Z, "Moment of Clarity," *The Black Album*, Roc-A-Fella Records, 2003.

19 Donald David, interview by author, July 2010.

20 Allison Samuels and David Gates, "Rap Takes Another Big Hit," *Newsweek*, December 5, 1999.

21 Samuel Maull, "Rapper Jay-Z Pleads Guilty to Assault in Knife Attack; Gets Probation," Associated Press, October 17, 2001.

22 Ellis Henican, "He Won't Let His Client Take the Rap," *Newsday*, December 5, 1999.

23 Samuel Maull, "Rapper Jay-Z Pleads Guilty to Assault in Knife Attack; Gets Probation," Associated Press, October 17, 2001.

24 Robert Sandall, "Destiny's Children," *Sunday Times*, August 9, 2009.

25 Jim Farber, "Rap for the Holidays," *New York Daily News*, January 6, 2000.

26 Recording Industry Association of America database, "Gold and Platinum (Jay-Z)," Recording Industry Association of America, http://www.riaa.com/goldandplatinumdata.php?table=SEARCH_RESULTS.

27 Bernie Resnick, telephone interview by author, October 2009.

28 Michael "MC Serch" Berrin, interview, December 2009.

29 Julia Boorstin, "What Makes Damon Dash?" *Fortune Small Business*, September 1, 2004.

30 Veronica Chambers, "The Playa," *New York Times*, September 22, 2002.

31 Julee Kaplan, "The Blueprint," *Women's Wear Daily*, November 30, 2009.

32 Veronica Chambers, "The Playa," *New York Times*, September 22, 2002.

33 Jay-Z, "U Don't Know," *The Blueprint*, Roc-A-Fella Records, 2001.

34 Rocawear staff, "About Rocawear," Rocawear Web site, http://www.rocawear.com/shop/aboutus.php.

35 Richard Harrington, "Jay-Z's Rhymes of Passion," *Washington Post*, January 2, 2000.

36 Touré, "The Book of Jay," *Rolling Stone*, December 15, 2005.

37 Denene Millner, "From Homeboys to Home Video," *New York Daily News*, September 29, 1998.

38 Kelefa Sanneh, "Gettin' Paid," *The New Yorker*, August 20, 2001.

39 David Connor, "Stars Get Rapped Up in Vodka," *Sun*, September 26, 2002.

Chapter 3: Building a Notorious Brand

1 MTV News staff, "Jay-Z's Yankee Memorabilia Is a Home Run, Fans Say," MTV News, August 31, 2010, mtv.com/news.

2 *XXL* Staff, "The Making of Reasonable Doubt," *XXL*, August 2006.

3 Jon Caramanica, "Jay-Z," in *The New Rolling Stone Album Guide, Ed. 4*, ed. Nathan Brackett and Christian Hoard (New York: Fireside, 2004), p. 424.

4 Jeff Chang, telephone interview by author, March 2010.

5 Rodolfo "DJ Clark Kent" Franklin, interview by author, January 2010.

6 Jonathan "Jaz-O" Burks, electronic message to author, June 2010.

7 Jay-Z, "Takeover," *The Blueprint*, Roc-A-Fella Records, 2001.

8 "Stillmatic," unreleased track that appeared only on the radio and later as part of a mix tape, 2001.

9 Jay-Z, "Takeover," *The Blueprint*, Roc-A-Fella Records, 2001.

10 Nasir "Nas" Jones, "Ether," *Stillmatic*, Ill Will/Columbia Records, 2001.

11 Jeff Chang, interview by author, March 2010.

12 Touré, "The Book of Jay," *Rolling Stone*, December 15, 2005.

13 Ibid.

14 Touré, telephone interview by author, December 2009.

15 Kelefa Sanneh, "Gettin' Paid," *The New Yorker*, August 20, 2001.

Chapter 4: Jay-Z's First Basketball Team

1 Jay-Z, "History," *Music Inspired by More Than a Game*, Zone 4/Interscope Records, 2009.

2 The Rucker staff, "History," The Rucker Web site, http://www.therucker.com/history.html.

3 Freddy "Fab Five" Brathwaite, interview by author, New York, New York, November 2009.

4 Dave Bry, "Look at Me Now," *XXL*, August 2005.

5 Tim Arango, "Reebok Running Up Sales with New Jay-Z Sneakers," *New York Post*, April 23, 2003.

6 Maureen Tkacik, "Hoops Phenom Nets $90 Million Deal with Nike," *Wall Street Journal*, May 23, 2003.

7 Sebastian Telfair, telephone interview by author, December 2009.

8 Jay-Z, "U Don't Know," *The Blueprint*, Roc-A-Fella Records, 2001.

9 Jamal Crawford, telephone interview by author, December 2009.

10 Jay-Z, "History," *Music Inspired by More Than a Game*, Zone 4/Interscope Records, 2009.

11 *Ad Age* staff, "10 Biggest Impact Madison + Vine Deals," *Advertising Age*, December 22, 2003.

Chapter 5: Early Retirement

1   *Fade to Black*, documentary, directed by Patrick Paulson and
     Michael John Warren (New York: Radical Media, 2004).

2   Jay-Z, "Encore," *The Black Album*, Roc-A-Fella Records, 2003.

3   Ibid.

4   Elizabeth Mendez Berry, "The Last Hustle," *Village Voice*,
     November 25, 2003.

5   Jon Caramanica, "Jay-Z," in *The New Rolling Stone Album
     Guide, Ed. 4*, ed. Nathan Brackett and Christian Hoard (New
     York: Fireside, 2004), p. 424.

6   David Edwards, "20 Crazy Facts," *Daily Mirror*, May 29,
     2006.

7   Recording Industry Association of America database, "Gold
     and Platinum (Jay-Z)," Recording Industry Association
     of America, http://www.riaa.com/goldandplatinumdata.
     php?table=SEARCH_RESULTS.

8   Ahmir "Questlove" Thompson, interview by author, January
     2010.

9   Touré, "Superstardom Is Boring: Jay-Z Quits (Again)," *New
     York Times*, November 16, 2003.

10   Jay-Z, "Excuse Me Miss," music video, directed by Julien
     Lutz, http://www.youtube.com/watch?v=tnDh0JhmaFw.

11   Richard Linnett, "An Urban Rite of Passage," *Advertising
     Age*, January 22, 2001.

12   Mark Binelli, "King of America," *Rolling Stone*, June 24, 2010.

13   Touré, "The Book of Jay," *Rolling Stone*, December 15, 2005.

14 Ibid.

15 Lola Ogunnaike, "Jay-Z, From Superstar to Suit," *New York Times*, August 28, 2005.

16 Touré, "The Book of Jay," *Rolling Stone*, December 15, 2005.

17 Lionel Deluy, "The Man Who Bling," *Independent*, July 9, 2006.

18 Dave Bry, "Look at Me Now," *XXL*, August 2005.

19 Tim Arango, "Dash to Finish," *New York Post*, May 9, 2005.

20 Alison Gendar, "A Dash of Violence at Upscale Magazine?" *New York Daily News*, October 4, 2005.

21 Touré, "The Book of Jay," *Rolling Stone*, December 15, 2005.

22 Bonsu Thompson, "'Bout Me," *XXL*, October 2009.

23 DeHaven Irby, interview by author, Brooklyn, New York, January 2010.

24 Jonathan "Jaz-O" Burks, telephone interview by author, May 2010.

25 Jay-Z, "Blueprint 2," *Blueprint 2: The Gift & The Curse*, Roc-A-Fella Records, 2002.

26 Jay-Z, "December 4th," *The Black Album*, Roc-A-Fella Records, 2003.

27 Jaz-O, "Ova," http://www.youtube.com/watch?v=kObkabiv0j8.

28 Jonathan "Jaz-O" Burks, interview by author, May 2010.

29 Rodolfo "DJ Clark Kent" Franklin, interview by author, January 2010.

30 Touré, "The Book of Jay," *Rolling Stone*, December 15, 2005.

31 Jay-Z, "Moment of Clarity," *The Black Album*, Roc-A-Fella Records, 2003.

Chapter 6: Def Jam Takeover

1   *Wall Street Journal* staff, "Seagram's Music Unit Nears
    Closing of Deal To Buy Out Def Jam," *Wall Street Journal*,
    March 1, 1999.

2   Mark Binelli, "King of America," *Rolling Stone*, June 24, 2010.

3   Touré, "The Book of Jay," *Rolling Stone*, December 15, 2005.

4   Ibid.

5   Jay-Z, "My 1st Song," *The Black Album*, Roc-A-Fella Records,
    2003.

6   Nick Simmons, interview by author, New York, New York,
    December 2009.

7   Bernie Resnick, telephone interview by author, October 2009.

8   Hillary Crosley, "Jay of All Trades," *Billboard*, December 2,
    2006.

9   Sylvia Patterson, "Singing in the Rain," *Observer*, August 26,
    2007.

10 Touré, "The Book of Jay," *Rolling Stone*, December 15, 2005.

11 Ibid.

12 Ahmir "Questlove" Thompson, telephone interview by
    author, January 2010.

13 Ahmir "Questlove" Thompson, telephone interview by
    author, February 2010.

14 Hillary Crosley, "Jay of All Trades," *Billboard*, December 2,
    2006.

15 Steve Jones, "This Week's Reviews," *USA Today*, August 28,
    2006.

16 Will Dukes, "Blood at the Roots," *Village Voice*, August 29, 2006.

17 Recording Industry Association of America database, "Gold and Platinum (Jay-Z)," Recording Industry Association of America, http://www.riaa.com/goldandplatinumdata.php?table=SEARCH_RESULTS.

18 Craig Kallman, telephone interview by author, June 2010.

19 Katie Hasty, "Nas Scores Third No. 1 Album with 'Hip-Hop Is Dead,'" *Billboard*, December 27, 2006.

20 Bonsu Thompson, "'Bout Me," *XXL*, October 2009 issue.

21 Jay-Z, "The Prelude," *Kingdom Come*, Roc-A-Fella Records, 2006.

22 Patrick "A Kid Called Roots" Lawrence, interview by author, November 2009.

23 Jay-Z, "Kingdom Come," *Kingdom Come*, Roc-A-Fella Records, 2006.

24 Peter Macia, Pitchfork Media, "Jay-Z: Kingdom Come," November 20, 2006, http://pitchfork.com/reviews/albums/9647-kingdom-come/.

25 Jay-Z, "Pray," *American Gangster*, Roc-A-Fella Records, 2007.

26 Kelefa Sanneh, "Jay-Z Finds Himself at the Movies," *New York Times*, November 5, 2007.

27 Rob Sheffield, "American Gangster," *Rolling Stone*, November 15, 2007, http://www.rollingstone.com/artists/jayz/albums/album/17121991/review/17139179/american_gangster.

28 *XXL* staff, "Time to Build," *XXL*, October 2009.

29 Mark Binelli, "King of America," *Rolling Stone*, June 24, 2010.

Chapter 7: Champagne Secrets

1   Branson Belchie, interview by author, New York, New York, February 2010.

2   Jay-Z, "Imaginary Players," *Vol. 1: In My Lifetime*, Roc-A-Fella Records, 1997.

3   Marcus Franklin, "Rapper Jay-Z Decides to Boycott Cristal," Associated Press, June 15, 2006.

4   Ibid.

5   Robin Givhan, "Bubbly Boycott? Oh Please, Jay-Z, Just Chill," *Washington Post*, July 7, 2006.

6   Mike Steinberger, "The Cristal Boycott," Slate, June 22, 2006, http://www.slate.com/id/2144328/.

7   Roberto Rogness, electronic message to author, February 2010.

8   Douglas Century, "Jay-Z Puts a Cap on Cristal," *New York Times*, July 2, 2006.

9   Adam Tschorn, "Night of 10,000 Bubbles," *Los Angeles Times*, December 30, 2007.

10 *Sunday Mail* staff, "Mariah's 30-K Carey-Out," *Sunday Mail*, April 3, 2005.

11 U.S. Patent and Trademark Office, "Armadale," U.S. Patent and Trademark Office database, http://tess2.uspto.gov/.

12 Ryan Schinman, interview by author, March 2010.

13 Burt Helm, "Is the Champagne in the Jay-Z Video for Real? It's Complicated," *BusinessWeek*, October 25, 2006, www .businessweek.com/the_thread/brandnewday/archives/ 2006/10/is_the_champagn.html.

14 Lyle Fass, interview by author, New York, New York, February 2010.

15 Philippe Bienvenu, telephone interview by author, February 2010.

16 Lyle Fass, interview by author, February 2010.

17 *Wine Spectator* staff, "Armand de Brignac," *Wine Spectator* members-only database, www.winespectator.com.

18 Esther-Mireya Tejeda, electronic message to author, April 2010.

19 Lyle Fass, interview by author, February 2010.

20 Isabelle Ruault, telephone interview by author, February 2010.

21 Kashif Thompson, telephone interview by author, February 2010.

22 Lyle Fass, interview by author, February 2010.

23 Sonia Murray, "Atlanta's Dupri Is a New-Style Mogul," *Atlanta Journal-Constitution*, September 26, 2004.

24 Greg Kelley, "French Bubbly Garners Hip-Hop Cred," *Wall Street Journal*, November 8, 2006.

25 Yvonne Lardner, interview by author, Chigny-Les-Roses, France, May 2010.

26 J. J. Battipaglia, telephone interview by author, August 2010.

27 Philippe Bienvenu, interviews by author, Chigny-Les-Roses, France, May 2010, and via telephone, February 2010.

28 U.S. Patent and Trademark Office, "Armand de Brignac," U.S. Patent and Trademark Office database, http://tess2.uspto.gov/.

29 Philippe Bienvenu, interview by author, February 2010.

30 Yvonne Lardner, electronic message to author, August 2010.

31 Lyle Fass, electronic messages to author, April 2010 and July 2010.

32 Esther-Mireya Tejeda, electronic message to author, April 2010.

33 Anonymous liquor industry source, electronic message to author, July 2010.

34 Lyle Fass, interview by author, February 2010.

Chapter 8: To Infinity—and Beyoncé

1 Kathy Ehrich and Tiffany McGee, "Source: Beyoncé and Jay-Z Take Out Marriage License," *People*, April 1, 2008, http://www.people.com/people/article/0,20187497,00.html.

2 Molly Friedman, "Beyoncé and Jay-Z Definitely, Maybe Getting Married Today," Gawker, April 4, 2008, http://defamer.gawker.com/376408/Beyoncé-and-jay+z-definitely-maybe-getting-married-today-you-decide.

3 TMZ staff, "We Are Sooooo Not Buying It," TMZ, April 4, 2008, http://www.tmz.com/2008/04/04/we-are-sooooo-not-buying-it/.

4 Jennifer Garcia and Mike Fleeman, "Source: Beyoncé and Jay-Z Are Married," April 4, 2008, http://www.people.com/people/article/0,20188764,00.html.

5 People.com staff, "Jay-Z and Beyoncé File Signed Marriage License," *People*, April 22, 2008, http://www.people.com/people/article/0,20194030,00.html.

6   Antoinette Y. Coulton, "Beyoncé Shows Off $5M Wedding Ring," *People*, September 6, 2008, http://www.people.com/people/article/0,20224021,00.html.

7   Jeff Chang, telephone interview by author, March 2010.

8   Mark Binelli, "King of America," *Rolling Stone*, June 24, 2010.

9   Jay-Z, "Girls, Girls, Girls," *The Blueprint*, Roc-A-Fella Records, 2001.

10 Geoff Boucher, "Destiny, Manifest," *Los Angeles Times*, July 1, 2001.

11 Tanith Carey, "God's Gift to Beyoncé," *Daily Mirror*, July 8, 2003.

12 Lisa Robinson, "Above and Beyoncé," *Vanity Fair*, November 1, 2005.

13 Tanith Carey, "God's Gift to Beyoncé," *Daily Mirror*, July 8, 2003.

14 Lisa Robinson, "Above and Beyoncé," *Vanity Fair*, November 1, 2005.

15 Jancee Dunn, "Date with Destiny," *Observer*, June 10, 2001.

16 Lisa Robinson, "Above and Beyoncé," *Vanity Fair*, November 1, 2005.

17 Ibid.

18 Tom Horan, "Dream Girl Beyoncé Has It All," *Telegraph Magazine*, November 8, 2008.

19 Jancee Dunn, "Date with Destiny," *Observer*, June 10, 2001.

20 Jonathan "Jaz-O" Burks, telephone interview by author, May 2010.

21 Jay-Z, "Big Pimpin'," *Vol. 3: Life and Times of S. Carter*, Roc-A-Fella Records, 1997.

22 Chenise Wilson, telephone interview by author, March 2010.

23 Cindy Pearlman, "Does Beyoncé Have Boyfriend in Her Destiny?" *Chicago Sun-Times*, July 17, 2002.

24 Adam Miller, "Eminem Discovering a Romantic 'Destiny,'" *New York Post*, April 15, 2001.

25 George Rush and Joanna Molloy, "Destined to Be?" *New York Daily News*, July 26, 2002.

26 Recording Industry Association of America database, "Gold and Platinum (Jay-Z)," Recording Industry Association of America, http://www.riaa.com/goldandplatinumdata.php?table=SEARCH_RESULTS.

27 Allison Samuels, "What Beyoncé Wants," *Newsweek*, July 29, 2002.

28 Touré, "The Book of Jay," *Rolling Stone*, December 15, 2005.

29 Lisa Robinson, "Above and Beyoncé," *Vanity Fair*, November 1, 2005.

30 Michael Hamersly, "Bye-bye for Jay-Z and Beyoncé," *Miami Herald*, March 16, 2003.

31 *Rolling Stone* staff, "100 Best Songs of the Decade," *Rolling Stone*, December 9, 2009, http://www.rollingstone.com/news/story/31248926/100_best_songs_of_the_decade/25.

32 Tanith Carey, "God's Gift to Beyoncé," *Daily Mirror*, July 8, 2003.

33 Lisa Robinson, "Above and Beyoncé," *Vanity Fair*, November 1, 2005.

34 Cathy McCabe, "Superstar Loves to Put the Booty In," *Daily Telegraph*, April 24, 2009.

35 Tom Horan, "Dream Girl Beyoncé Has It All," *Telegraph Magazine*, November 8, 2008.

36 Lisa Robinson, "Above and Beyoncé," *Vanity Fair*, November 1, 2005.

37 Larry King, "Interview with Beyoncé," *Larry King Live* transcript, November 26, 2009.

38 Lacey Rose, telephone interview by author, April 2010.

39 Bernie Resnick, telephone interview by author, October 2009.

40 Touré, "The Book of Jay," *Rolling Stone*, December 15, 2005.

41 Jeff Chang, telephone interview by author, March 2010.

42 Jeff Chang, interview by author, March 2010.

43 Ryan Schinman, telephone interview by author, March 2010.

44 Beyoncé, "Upgrade U," *B'Day*, Music World/Columbia Records, 2006.

45 Terry Pristin, "Out of the Kitchen and into the Shopping Mall," *New York Times*, October 25, 2006.

46 Lacey Rose, interview by author, April 2010.

47 James "Jim Jonsin" Scheffer, interview by author, Los Angeles, California, January 2010.

48 Lacey Rose, interview by author, April 2010.

49 Ryan Schinman, interview by author, March 2010.

Chapter 9: Net Gain

1 Ohm Youngmisuk, "No Sleep Till Brooklyn," *New York Daily News*, November 13, 2005.

2   Robert Caro, telephone interview by author, April 2009; Michael Shapiro, telephone interview by author, April 2009. Note: Excerpts from these interviews appeared in my article "Who Framed Walter O'Malley," *Forbes*, April 14, 2009, http://www.forbes.com/2009/04/14/brooklyn-dodgers-stadium-lifestyle-sports-baseball-stadiums.html.

3   Charles V. Bagli, "A Grand Plan in Brooklyn for the Nets' Arena Complex," *New York Times*, December 11, 2003.

4   David Porter, "Nets Reach Deal to Sell Team to Brooklyn Developer," Associated Press, January 22, 2004.

5   Ohm Youngmisuk, "No Sleep Till Brooklyn," *New York Daily News*, November 13, 2005.

6   Paul Swangard, telephone interview by author, May 2010.

7   Ibid.

8   Paul Suwan, "Nets Greeted by Warm Welcome," *Journal News*, January 24, 2004.

9   Frank DiGiacomo with Carson Griffith, "Hip-Hop Mogul Jay-Z Upset..." *New York Daily News*, July 28, 2010.

10   Catherine Curan, "Jay-Z's 99 Problems," *New York Post*, May 16, 2010, http://www.nypost.com/p/news/business/jay_NJOKUMG5lyyYswtQo2zrJL/0.

11   Ohm Youngmisuk, "No Sleep Till Brooklyn," *New York Daily News*, November 13, 2005.

12   Kurt Badenhausen, telephone interview by author, May 2010.

13   Ibid.

14   Touré, "The Book of Jay," *Rolling Stone*, December 15, 2005.

15   Ohm Youngmisuk, "No Sleep Till Brooklyn," *New York Daily News*, November 13, 2005.

16 Ibid.

17 ESPN staff, "NBA Attendance Report—2010," *ESPN*, http://
espn.go.com/nba/attendance/_/order/false.

18 Julia Vitullo-Martin, "Cross Country: A Hole Grows in
Brooklyn," *Wall Street Journal*, March 7, 2009.

19 Matthew Futterman, "Bruce Ratner's NBA Waterloo," *Wall
Street Journal*, May 11, 2010.

20 Anita Raghavan, "Last Man Standing," *Forbes*, March 30,
2009.

21 Matthew Futterman, "Bruce Ratner's NBA Waterloo," *Wall
Street Journal*, May 11, 2010.

22 Rebecca Rosenberg, Fred Kerber, and Lukas I. Alpert, "Nets'
New Owner Dines with Mayor Bloomberg, Jay-Z," *New York
Post*, May 20, 2010.

23 Thomas J. Sheeran, "Cleveland Fans to LeBron: Please,
Please Stay," Associated Press, May 18, 2010.

24 Julian Garcia, "Nets Fire 1st Shot," *New York Daily News*,
July 1, 2010.

25 Jonathan Abrams, "Nets, Through Owner, Ask Fans to Be
Patient," *New York Times*, July 13, 2010.

26 Kevin Armstrong, "Cases Made in King's Court," *New York
Daily News*, July 2, 2010.

27 Jeff Kearns, "Waiting on LeBron Drives Madison Square
Options," *Bloomberg*, July 7, 2010, http://www.bloomberg.
com/news/2010-07-07/waiting-on-lebron-drives-madison-
square-garden-options-chart-of-the-day.html.

28 Howard Beck and Jonathan Abrams, "James Picks Miami,
Ending NBA's Suspense," *New York Times*, July 9, 2010.

29 Jonathan Abrams, "Nets, Through Owner, Ask Fans to Be Patient," *New York Times*, July 13, 2010.

30 Rich Calder, "Markowitz: LeBron Might Be Taking 'Vacation' in Miami Before Joining Brooklyn Nets," *New York Post*, July 9, 2010.

31 Ibid.

Chapter 10: Who Killed the Jay-Z Jeep?

1 Michael "Serch" Berrin, telephone interview by author, December 2009.

2 Dorothy Pomerantz and Lacey Rose, "The Celebrity 100," *Forbes*, June 28, 2010, http://www.forbes.com/2010/06/22/lady-gaga-oprah-winfrey-business-entertainment-celeb-100-10_land.html.

3 Motorola Media Center, telephone and electronic messages by author, April 2010.

4 Lola Ogunnaike, "Steve Stoute Would Like to Turn You into a Sneaker," *Rolling Stone*, December 15, 2005.

5 Lisa Eisner, "Private Lives: Adrian Van Anz," *Vanity Fair*, April 2009.

6 Craig McLean, "The Bling Philanthropist," *Daily Telegraph*, November 18, 2006.

7 Julie Creswell, "Nothing Sells Like Celebrity," *New York Times*, June 22, 2008.

8 Touré, "The Book of Jay," *Rolling Stone*, December 15, 2005.

9 Marques McCammon, interview by author, Vista, California, March 2010.

10 LL Cool J, "Big Ole Butt," *Walking with a Panther*, Def Jam/ Columbia/CBS Records, 1989.

11 Michael "Serch" Berrin, telephone interview by author, June 2010.

12 Michael "Serch" Berrin, telephone interview by author, December 2009.

13 CNN Money staff, "Iacocca Teams with Snoop Dogg," CNN Money, August 5, 2005, money.cnn.com.

14 Alison Gendar, "A Dash of Violence at Upscale Magazine?" *New York Daily News*, October 4, 2005.

15 United States Securities and Exchange Commission staff, "Form 8-K: Iconix Group," United States Securities and Exchange Commission, March 5, 2007.

16 Greg Weisman, telephone interview by author, April 2010.

17 United States Securities and Exchange Commission staff, "Form 8-K: Iconix Group," United States Securities and Exchange Commission, March 5, 2007.

18 Ken Thomas, "General Motors, Jay-Z Join Forces on SUV Concept," Associated Press, January 6, 2007.

19 Marques McCammon, interview by author, March 2010.

20 U.S. Patent and Trademark Office staff, "Jay-Z Blue," U.S. Patent and Trademark Office database, accessed April 2010, http://tess2.uspto.gov/.

21 Michael "Serch" Berrin, interview by author, June 2010.

22 Peter Martin, "Don't Blame the Industry," *Financial Times*, February 28, 2002.

23 Ryan Schinman, interview by author, March 2010.

24 *Global Grind* staff, ". . . Jiggaman's Jeep," *Global Grind*, January 19, 2010, http://globalgrind.com/source/bossip. com/1309150/photos-from-a-maybach-to-a-jeep/.

25 Jay-Z feat. Swizz Beatz, "On to the Next One," *The Blueprint 3*, Roc Nation, 2009.

Chapter 11: Reinventing the Roc

1 Nielsen Company staff, "2009 Year-End Music Industry Report," Nielsen Company, 2009.

2 Mariel Concepcion, "Jay-Z: He's a Business, Man," *Billboard*, July 25, 2009.

3 Mark Binelli, "King of America," *Rolling Stone*, June 24, 2010.

4 *Billboard* staff, "Jay-Z to Step Down as Def Jam President," *Billboard*, December 24, 2007.

5 Ibid.

6 Mariel Concepcion, "Jay-Z: He's a Business, Man," *Billboard*, July 25, 2009.

7 Donald David, interview by author, July 2010.

8 Jeff Leeds, "In Rapper's Deal, A New Model for Music Business," *New York Times*, April 3, 2008.

9 Richard Harrington, "Jay-Z's Rhymes of Passion," *Washington Post*, January 2, 2000.

10 Ray Waddell, "Rolling Stones Tour Grosses More Than Half a Billion," *Billboard*, October 3, 2007.

11 Nielsen Company staff, "2009 Year-End Music Industry Report," Nielsen Company, 2009.

12 Kelley L. Carter, "Jay-Z: The Free Press Interview," *Detroit Free Press*, November 19, 2004.

13 Golnar Motevalli, "Jay-Z Wins Over Doubters at Glastonbury," Reuters, June 30, 2008.

14 Peter Kafka, "The Road to Riches," *Forbes*, July 7, 2003.

15 Note: This comment is based on tour data from Pollstar Pro.

16 Jeff Chang, interview by author, March 2010.

17 Dina LaPolt and Bernie Resnick, "Multiple Rights Deals in the U.S.: 360 and Beyond," excerpted from *Multiple Rights Deals in the Music Industry*, January 2009.

18 Stephen E. Siwek, "The True Cost of Sound Recording Piracy to the U.S. Economy," Institute for Policy Innovation, August 2007.

19 Swati Pandey, "Stocks, Options, and Rock 'n Roll," *Los Angeles Times*, Company Town blog, October 17, 2008, http://latimesblogs.latimes.com/entertainmentnewsbuzz/2008/10/u2-live-nation.html.

20 Dina LaPolt, telephone interview by author, November 2009.

21 Bernie Resnick, telephone interview by author, October 2010.

22 Rob Markman, "Hand It Down," *XXL*, October 2009.

23 Nick Simmons, interview by author, December 2009.

24 Elizabeth Mendez Berry, interview by author, May 2010.

Chapter 12: History and Beyond

1 Catherine Curan, "Jay-Z's 99 Problems," *New York Post*, May 16, 2010.

2 Craig Kallman, telephone interview by author, June 2010.

3   Robert Sandall, "Destiny's Children," *Sunday Times*, August 9, 2009.

4   Baz Bamigboye, "Coming to Town: Jay-Z and a Very Lucky Fela," *Daily Mail*, March 19, 2010, http://www.dailymail. co.uk/tvshowbiz/article-1259038/Beyoncés-husband-Jay-Z-lucky-Fela.html.

5   *Daily Mail* staff, "Jay-Z Hints at Arsenal Investment as Rap Superstar Admits He Fell Crazy in Love with Gunners Thanks to Thierry Henry," *Daily Mail*, March 23, 2010, http://www.dailymail.co.uk/sport/football/article-1259957/ Jay-Z-hints-Arsenal-investment-rap-star-admits-fell-Crazy-Love-Gunners-thanks-Thierry-Henry.html.

6   Jay-Z, "History," *Music Inspired by More Than a Game*, Zone 4/Interscope Records, 2009.

7   Rodolfo "DJ Clark Kent" Franklin, interview by author, Brooklyn, New York, January 2010.

INDEX